Supporting Children with Dyslexia

Practical Approaches for Teachers and Parents

2nd Edition

Garry Squires and Sally McKeown

continuum

Continuum International Publishing Group

The Tower Building	80 Maiden Lane
11 York Road	Suite 704
London	New York
SE1 7NX	NY 10038

www.continuumbooks.com

First published by Questions Publishing Company Ltd 2003
Second edition published by Continuum 2006

Design by: James Davies
Illustrations by: Iqbal Aslam
Cover photogaraph by: Amanda Greeley
With thanks to staff and children at Leasowes Community College

British Library Cataloguing-in-Publication Data
A catalogue record for this book is available from the British Library.

ISBN: 0–8264–8078–0 (paperback)

Library of Congress Cataloging-in-Publication Data
Squires, Garry.
Supporting children with dyslexia : practical approaches for teachers and parents / Garry Squires and Sally McKeown. – 2nd ed.
    p. cm.
Includes bibliographical references and index.
ISBN 0–8264–8078–0 (pbk.)
1. Dyslexic children – Education – Great Britain. I.
McKeown, Sally. II. Title. LC4710.G7568 2006
371.91'44–dc22 2006000271

Typeset by BookEns Ltd, Royston, Hertfordshire
Printed and bound in Great Britain by The Bath Press, Bath

Contents

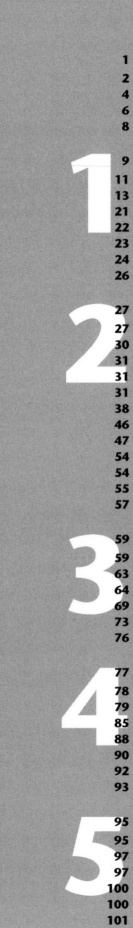

Introduction

Dyslexia is a term used to describe people who have specific difficulties in learning to read, write and spell. It may be neurological in origin and can often have associated difficulties with memory and sequential thinking. Dyslexia is not new – it has been around for as long as people have endeavoured to read and write and has been recognized as a difficulty in developing these skills since it was first described by James Kerr and W.M. Morgan in 1896 (see box below). Likewise, compulsory schooling has been around for well over a hundred years and has always had an emphasis on literacy – potentially disadvantaging dyslexic pupils. It is likely that every present-day classroom will have four or five children who have a degree of dyslexia.

> Morgan described a case of a 14-year-old boy, Percy F. He described him as a *'bright and intelligent boy, quick at games, and in no way inferior to others of his age'*.
>
> He went on to describe Percy's unexpected difficulty with reading: *'His great difficulty has been – and is now – his ability to learn to read. This inability is so remarkable, and so pronounced, that I have no doubt it is due to some congenital defect'*.
>
> Morgan highlighted that this was not due to poor teaching. *'He has been at school or under tutors since he was 7 years old, and the greatest efforts have been made to teach him to read, but, in spite of this laborious and persistent training, he can only with difficulty spell out words of one syllable.'*
>
> He gives an example of Percy's spelling: ***'Now, you word me wale I spin if. Calfuly winder the sturng rond the Pag'***. [Now, you watch me while I spin it. Carefully winding the string round the peg.]
>
> Morgan, W.M. (1896) A Case of Congenital Word Blindness. *The British Medical Journal.*

What do you do with dyslexic children?

There are plenty of books about dyslexia and well-structured teaching packs that focus on the remediation of difficulties. But not much is written about the day-to-day work that goes on in mainstream classrooms or about how parents can help. This book sets out to address this issue by providing an understanding of what it is like to be dyslexic and giving ideas that focus on the solutions to problems that may be encountered. This 2nd edition of *Supporting Children with Dyslexia* now offers even more information, particularly on the definitions of dyslexia, perceptual issues, spelling patterns, remedial programmes and progress, useful technologies, and dyscalculia.

Inclusion of dyslexic children

The term 'dyslexia' evokes anxiety and uncertainty for some teachers who hear it being used to describe a child with whom they have contact. Equally, parents worry that if their child is dyslexic then they can only be taught successfully by a 'specialist' teacher (who has a qualification in teaching dyslexic children). Anecdotal examples of this from an Educational Psychologist include:

One child had made tremendous progress on small step targets for literacy set on his individual education programme (IEP), yet his class teacher continued to comment in a negative way about how he was not able to do any better in class. A very successful remedial programme had led to an increase in literacy skills yet somehow this was not seen as helpful to the teacher. What could be done to lead to an improvement in performance in class? How could the class teacher be helped to support the child more effectively in day-to-day classroom work?

Work with a child with reading difficulties had resulted in Statutory Assessment being undertaken and a Statement of Special Educational Needs had been produced offering support. A few days later the parent telephoned me and was quite concerned; her son's class teacher had made a comment that she did not know anything about dyslexia.

(Squires, 2001c)

The Code of Practice for Special Educational Needs (DfES, 2001) provides guidance for working with pupils who have a wide range of educational needs including dyslexia. The Code of Practice promotes inclusion and sets out an expectation that children with special educational needs will normally have their needs met in a mainstream school and have access to a broad and balanced National Curriculum. In terms of dyslexia this means that schools need to understand what it is like to be dyslexic and what can be done to facilitate learning for these pupils. A number of local education authorities have embarked on raising awareness of dyslexia in schools to help them become more 'dyslexia friendly' with accreditation from the British Dyslexia Association (BDA).

The Mission Statement from the BDA sets out the inclusion agenda for dyslexic children:

> *The aim of the Dyslexia-Friendly LEAs Initiative and the associated BDA Quality Mark is to promote excellent practice by the LEA as it carries out its role of supporting and challenging its schools to improve accessibility to learning for more children.*

A dyslexia-friendly school would be one that is able to recognize and help remediate difficulties that a child may have with reading and spelling. It would also respond to other difficulties that the child presents and would look for ways to present the curriculum so that the child could access it. Consideration would be given to helping children record their ideas and to express themselves. The school would think about how to improve the classroom environment and how to work well with parents and outside agencies.

Details of how LEAs can become Dyslexia Friendly are given on the BDA website: www.bdadyslexia.org.uk/extra210.html

Teachers are skilled professionals who already have a range of strategies that are helpful to dyslexic children. By constantly updating their resources and seeking support from SENCos (Special Educational Needs Co-ordinators) and outside specialists, they successfully deal with an ever-increasing range of diagnosed difficulties in their classrooms. One role for this book is to help teachers reflect on, and become more skilled in dealing with, individual differences by considering alternative approaches to enhancing their teaching skills. It has been argued that reflection leads to greater awareness of what 'constitutes appropriate pedagogic practice' (Kullman, 1998) and encourages personal development (Bulstrode and Hunt, 2000). Conversation is seen as an important way of making sense of teaching experiences, and as a means of exchanging ideas and new ways to act in the classroom (Stanulis and Russell, 2000). This book is presented as a catalyst for reflection, discussion and development as well as being a source of ideas and strategies.

Some of this material has previously been given in booklet form to teachers and has enabled them to consider how best to meet individual needs and help dyslexic pupils to achieve. Such an approach helps to contribute towards an inclusive ethos of dyslexia-friendly schools. As one teacher said:

'Using these ideas has helped me recognize what I do already, it has given me some new ideas ... it has helped me feel more confident and it has helped my pupil be more confident in class.'

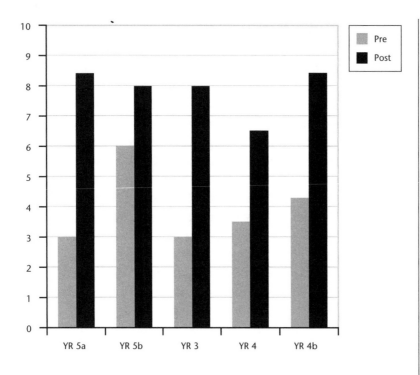

Changes in teacher
confidence ratings when
given information about
dyslexia (Squires, 2001a)

Making a graduated response

The Code of Practice recognizes that there is a continuum of special educational needs. The dyslexia spectrum runs from pupils with severe dyslexia, who find print very intimidating and need a high level of support, to those who are able to record their ideas in writing but whose spelling is somewhat idiosyncratic. This means that teachers will have to notice what children find difficult and then respond by modifying their teaching – this is the principle of early intervention. The responsibility for meeting a child's special educational needs rests with the class teacher. Advice may be sought from other specialists or from the SENCo. This allows the school to make a graduated response – those children who need the most help are able to receive it while those who need the least are encouraged to work independently.

The Code of Practice sets out three levels of support:

- *School Action* – the steps that the class teacher, SENCo and school can take to provide support.
- *School Action Plus* – the school seeks additional advice from outside agencies (advisory teachers, speech and language therapists, occupational therapists, educational psychologists, etc.).
- *Statement of Special Educational Needs* – the child's needs are considered to be long term and complex and requiring more than has been provided at School Action and School Action Plus.

Schools can request Statutory Assessment, and best practice is contained in the Code of Practice Toolkit section called 'Writing Advice'. The LEA will usually request all relevant records, including evidence that

IEPs have been designed and implemented in attempting to meet the needs of the child. The information will include records of the pupil's progress in the National Curriculum and any standardized test results. The LEA will then decide whether or not to proceed with the assessment, which will involve an Educational Psychologist and a medical report as well as input from any other agencies involved with the child (e.g. social services). Parents' views have to be considered too. The issuing of a Statement should take a maximum of six months and it must then be reviewed annually and at school transfer time. Statements issued to dyslexic children usually specify a certain amount of specialist support and can trigger special consideration in exams, such as extra time or the help of an amanuensis.

There is currently a move away from Statementing. The Audit Commission produced a report in 2002 that commented on the rising numbers of Statements of SEN and questioned the process. The report highlighted Statementing as a bureaucratic and costly process that diverts energy and money away from children. Since that report there has been greater emphasis on 'early intervention' and many LEAs have started to explore how to delegate money directly to schools so that help can be given to children without the need for a Statement.

This change is not without tensions. On the one hand schools are expected to follow an achievement agenda and are judged by their SATs results and are therefore likely to want to focus their efforts on higher achieving pupils. This agenda is supported through the allocation of additional resources to those pupils who just miss the levels set for their age. Small remedial group work is offered to pupils in literacy and numeracy through ELS (Early Literacy Support); ALS (Additional Literacy Support), FLS (Further Literacy Support) and Springboard (numeracy booster lessons). On the other hand, schools are being asked to be more inclusive and to focus efforts on children who will not achieve the expected levels in SATs at the end of each Key Stage. These children are supported through the Code of Practice for SEN procedures and though Wave 2 and 3 interventions. Advice is being given to schools on a regular basis from the DfES and includes:

- *The National Numeracy Strategy. The daily mathematics lesson: Guidance to support pupils with dyslexia and dyscalculia* Ref DfES 0512/2001
- *Early Literacy Support* Ref DfES 0652/2001
- *Key Stage 3 National Strategy. Literacy progression unit: Writing Organisation* Ref DfES 0473/2001
- *Key Stage 3 National Strategy. Literacy progression unit: Spelling* Ref DfES 0475/2001
- *Key Stage 3 National Strategy. Literacy progression unit: Phonics* Ref DfES 0477/2001
- *The National Literacy and Numeracy Strategies. Including all children in the literacy hour and daily mathematics lesson: Management Guide Folder* Ref DfES 0465/2002

- *The National Literacy Strategy. Targeting support: choosing and implementing interventions for children with significant literacy difficulties* Ref DfES 0201/2003
- *Playing with sounds* Ref DfES 0280-2004
- *Teaching and learning for children with SEN in the primary years* Ref DfES 0321-2004
- *Supporting children with gaps in their mathematical understanding: Wave 3 mathematics* Ref DfES 1168-2005 G
- *Learning and teaching for dyslexic children* CDROM package. Ref DfES1184-2005CDI

The tension between the inclusion agenda and the achievement agenda is partially resolved by thinking about the achievement of all children. This is set out in the government documents *Removing Barriers to Achievement* (Ref DfES 0117/2004) and *Every Child Matters* (DfES, 2003). Five themes are now identified for supporting children with implications for thinking about dyslexia:

- *Be healthy* e.g. does the child have a positive self-esteem and self-image? Are they coping with school at an emotional level?
- *Stay safe* e.g. does the child recognize danger in their environment? Can they make sense of warning signs? Are they able to plan and manage their time and actions safely? Is the child supported in taking risks with learning?
- *Enjoy and achieve* e.g. is the child able to make progress? Can they access the curriculum? Can they demonstrate learning?
- *Make a positive contribution* e.g. can the child contribute to the school community?
- *Achieve economic well-being* e.g. how are they being supported through the examination system? Is careers guidance available?

These changes in education mean that many LEAs will be looking for alternative ways to Statementing for providing support to dyslexic children. This will include improving the skills of mainstream teachers and teaching assistants. It is generally referred to as 'capacity building' – improving the whole school's capacity to meet the needs of all pupils by increasing teaching skills. This is the principle behind 'dyslexia-friendly' initiatives and behind this book.

Parents as equal partners

The Code of Practice values the role of parents as equal in status to that of teachers and other professionals. It recognizes that parents have a vital part to play in contributing to how their children's educational needs can be met.

- Parents are experts about what it is like to live with their children. Parents can contribute important information about the problems facing the child at home – perhaps the dyslexic child struggles for hours to complete homework that is expected to take other children in his or her class 20 minutes. Parents will have developed strategies for supporting the child's organization or for checking that they understand instructions when they are told to do something. Parents will know many of the child's strengths and weaknesses and can help by sharing with staff their solutions to day-to-day problems that exist at home, which can be transferred into school.

- Parents will have personal resources and time that they can commit to supporting the child. These will depend on:
  - how much patience a person has;
  - how well they can read or write;
  - how good their rapport is with their children;
  - how well they are able to explain things;
  - the extent to which they can encourage and motivate the child;
  - how anxious they feel about their child's progress;
  - how well they are able to deal with the child's worries and frustrations.
- There is some evidence to suggest that dyslexia might run in families. If this is the case, the parents might themselves have faced and solved the problems now facing the child. Questions such as 'What works for you?' or 'How do you remember things?' may provide valuable insights into finding ways of supporting the child.
- Parents can help with monitoring and can carry out simple remedial programmes under the guidance of the class teacher.

Many schools encourage parents to participate through regular meetings with teaching staff and/or support staff. The Code of Practice recommends that when a child has an identified special educational need, parents and school should review progress together at least twice a year (one time might be part of a normal parental consultation evening). Some schools run courses to help parents develop specific skills to support their children.

Summary

- Dyslexic children are found in mainstream classrooms and it is expected that they will be included in a broad and balanced curriculum. The responsibility for their teaching lies with their class teacher. Teachers can work with the SENCo or outside agencies.

- Schools and parents want access to information to help them understand the needs of dyslexic children and how they can be supported in mainstream classes. In recent years there has been a lot of information sent to schools to help them work more effectively with dyslexic children.

- Teachers and teaching assistants already have a range of skills and expertise and can draw upon more from support agencies and outside specialists.

- Parents have a valuable contribution to make and schools have a responsibility to involve parents as equal partners.

- There is a continuum of dyslexia and a graduated response can be made to help the child become an independent learner.

- There needs to be a focus on solutions so that the presenting problems are not seen as being insurmountable.

1 | Definitions and Challenges

Teachers frequently encounter children with reading and spelling difficulties and need to consider how best to support them across the curriculum. A survey involving over fifty schools in ten local education authorities found evidence of good practice when looking at how pupils with Statements for specific learning difficulties were progressing in reading, spelling and writing (Ofsted, 1999). However, when teachers are asked about how confident they feel about teaching dyslexic children, they do not always respond as would be expected. They seem to see dyslexic children as having greatly different needs to other 'common or garden' poor readers or poor spellers. Teachers were asked to describe children with reading and writing difficulties and they were asked to define dyslexia. Their responses are tabled below:

Constructs used by teachers (Squires, 2001a)

Dyslexia concept	Overlap	Literacy difficulty concept
• many aspects/traits ← → single difficulty	• trouble with reading, writing and spelling	• lack of experience of reading
• different types of dyslexia	• not being able to decode symbols	• poor phonological skills
• problems with rote learning		• poor behaviour due to frustration
• confusion with textual information		• low confidence
• sequencing difficulties		• dependent learning style/teacher reliant
• intelligence		• poor quality of work
• neurological processing difficulty		• slow
• good oral/aural but poor written		• thinks everything is wrong
• poor concentration		• hard to motivate
		• restricted vocabulary when writing

There appears very little overlap between the two concepts being constructed by teachers. Maybe this is because there are many definitions of dyslexia, each one emphasizing slightly different features or views about the nature and causes of the difficulties. This leads to some confusion and then teachers become uncertain about what to do.

What hypotheses are there about the causes of dyslexia?

The word 'dyslexia' conjures up many things to many people. There are numerous definitions around, each with a slightly different emphasis. It is no surprise therefore that there is no simple test for dyslexia.

One thing that all the different definitions have in common is that dyslexia is a difficulty with reading or spelling that cannot be accounted for by other explanations. Part of the assessment of dyslexia involves trying to rule out other possible causes of poor reading or poor spelling.

What follows is a brief description of each of the main hypotheses. In practical terms we cannot tell directly whether a pupil has a particular neurological problem, whether it is a cognitive weakness or whether some crucial learning has not taken place. We need to consider all the hypotheses and build up a pattern of strengths and weaknesses for a particular pupil. These different hypotheses should guide us in determining the kinds of things to assess:

- *Dyslexia is a phonological processing difficulty* related to more general language processing problems. This suggests that difficulties in the way that sound is perceived and processed interferes with learning how sound is represented in written language. Children will have poor phonological awareness, difficulty in repeating polysyllabic words, less sensitivity to alliteration and rhyme than peers; difficulty with rapidly naming objects; poor short-term memory tasks, e.g. poor skills at making Spoonerisms from two given words.
- *Dyslexia is visual processing difficulty.* An inability to achieve a stable image of the word, to track accurately, to suppress eye-movement between fixing on groups of letters or to process shape, orientation or relationships between visual elements makes distinguishing between letters and words more difficult.
- Dyslexia is a difficulty related to how the brain processes similar frequencies and this interferes with distinguishing similar sounds and quickly changing patterns of letters as the eye scans words. In research this is referred to as the *transient magnocellular deficit hypothesis.*
- Dyslexia is a problem concerning the way that attention is allocated to tasks. The child may put too much emphasis on decoding letters and words and too little on understanding the communication. Or the child may not be able to hold information well in working memory while shifting attention between the tasks of decoding letter sounds and blending. There are two different hypotheses concerned with attentional control. The first is the *executive control deficit hypothesis*; this suggests that there is difficulty integrating information from different sensory

pathways. The second is the *balance model of reading*; this suggests that some children focus too much on the meaning of the text while others focus too much on the perceptual aspects.

- Dyslexia is the result of a complex skill *not becoming automatic*. Poor automatization of early articulation skills, eye-movements and auditory skills interferes with reading fluidity and leads to laboured reading.
- Reading and spelling require the development of different strategies at different ages. *Dyslexic children do not learn new strategies easily* or become over-reliant on earlier learned but less efficient strategies. This explanation is partly related to the complexity of the English language and the need for orthographic and morphological strategies to develop to deal with non-phonologically regular words.

These explanations arise partly from the starting perspective of the researchers and the way in which they define dyslexia and select participants for their investigations. However:

- Each hypothesis is supported by research evidence.
- Different parts of the brain are implicated.
- A range of cognitive profiles is evident when test scores are examined.
- Developmental processes influence ocular stability and control, speech production and phonological awareness, motor control and co-ordination, and ability to respond to the level of textual information.

This leads to the view that dyslexia is a collection of conditions characterized by poor reading and/or poor spelling with a number of cognitive processes involved that produce different patterns of strengths and weaknesses in different children (Squires, 2003).

There are some overlaps from the different causal hypotheses to the kinds of behaviours that children will exhibit in reading and consequently to the kinds of things that we could assess. With so many cognitive processes being involved in reading and spelling, a weakness in any one could lead to difficulties in successfully completing literacy tasks. The difficulties in cognitive processing of information are likely to lead to problems in other aspects of life. Assessment can focus on trying to understand difficulties so that help can be targeted to supporting difficulties, remediation of weaknesses or adapting the learning environment to promote inclusion.

Different definitions of dyslexia

The working party of the British Psychological Society (BPS) (1999) has offered a broad definition of dyslexia:

Dyslexia is evident when accurate and fluent word reading and/or spelling develops very incompletely or with great difficulty. This focuses on literacy learning at the 'word level' and implies that the problem is severe and persistent despite appropriate learning opportunities. It provides the basis for a staged process of assessment through teaching.

The definition emphasizes:

- a lack of accuracy in reading or spelling;
- a lack of fluency when reading or spelling;
- a problem at the 'word level' of the National Literacy Strategy;
- the need for appropriate teaching;
- the severity and persistence of the difficulties;
- an interaction between teaching and learning.

The BPS definition is not exclusive and this means that any child with literacy difficulties that are severe and persistent and not responsive to well-structured, frequently provided remedial teaching could be considered as being dyslexic. This means that care has to be taken if there are better descriptive labels that could encompass more complex difficulties. This lack of distinction is useful in that it reminds us that all children with literacy difficulties need the same kind of teaching to help them overcome these difficulties.

Some people suggest that dyslexia is organic in origin. Many definitions include an unexpected inability of the child to develop literacy skills despite good teaching. This type of definition is sometimes referred to as a 'discrepancy definition' and leads to the view that children can only be dyslexic if they are bright. Some definitions focus on the linguistic aspects (e.g. Heaton and Winterson, 1996; Rack, 1994). Others offer a definition that takes into account a core problem and a collection of associated difficulties (e.g. Turner, 1997). Some definitions describe the core problems as being related to how the brain is able to make repeated actions fluent by making them automatic (e.g. Nicholson *et al.*, 1995, Nicholson *et al.*, 1999).

These other definitions outline a range of associated factors:

- difficulties with short-term memory capacity;
- difficulties with working memory;
- phonological difficulties (e.g. difficulty with sound awareness);
- visual difficulties (see page 14);
- perceptual difficulties;
- an unexpected difference between performance in some areas and performance in literacy;
- a slow speed in noticing, processing and responding to information;
- poor organizational skills and planning skills;
- a lack of fluency;
- difficulty with automaticity.

For some children there are additional difficulties. They may:

- become over-reliant on adult support;
- become reluctant to try, even when the task is well within their capability;
- have low self-esteem and feelings of low self-worth;
- avoid academic tasks, particularly those involving reading or writing;
- develop emotional and behavioural difficulties.

Perceptual issues

Multisensory skills

Reading and writing rely upon a number of perceptual processes for successful and automatic performance. The visual system is involved in looking at words (either in text, or those that we have produced in writing). Patterns of light that fall on the back of the eye are then built up into recognizable shapes and we are able to decode words and access meaning. Similarly, when we read out loud (or quietly to ourselves using the inner voice), we have to understand the sound systems in English so that we can 'hear' what we read. As we spell each word, we can hear the sounds and combine them to form the words that we want. When we write, we can use muscle memory to help us 'feel' whether each word is spelt correctly. This makes literacy a multi-sensory experience for most competent readers.

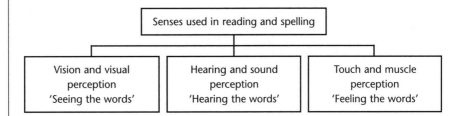

The visual system and the phonological system have their own lexicon and can access the meaning of words independently of each other (Waldie and Mosley, 2000). This means that it is possible to read without accessing sound directly. Speed-reading, scanning and skimming are examples of this advanced reading skill. A whole book can be read in a matter of seconds if the reader simply wants to find a particular piece of information and access to all the meaning of the text is not required.

Each of the three systems are sophisticated and have evolved over millions of years. None of the systems have evolved specifically with reading and writing in mind. This means that some people may have perceptual systems that are adequate for everyday use but which have imperfections or faults that impair reading or spelling acquisition and can contribute to dyslexia. A child with a perceptual difficulty will adapt to their environment by becoming more reliant on other senses and this leads to development of preferred learning styles. It is possible to identify strengths and weaknesses and then decide whether to:

- Teach to strengths as this is likely to be the style that the child finds easiest for learning and will help motivation. Teaching focuses on building up skills and learning mnemonic tricks and strategies to get around difficulties. The downside is that weaknesses remain unremediated.
- Teach to weaknesses to build up perceptual skills and processing by encouraging more effort and potentially the development of weaker neurological pathways. Some evidence for this is apparent in studies of neural pathways in the corpus collasum in musicians (Schlaug *et al.*, 1995). The difficulty with this approach is that children find it hard to work to weaknesses and can become demotivated and engage in task avoidance.
- Teach in a multi-sensory way and combine the best aspects of both. The child is able to utilize strengths for part of the learning (finding some parts of the work easy and being motivated by this). At the same time, part of the learning attempts to develop skills that are weak. Although teaching is multi-sensory, to be effective it will not be the same for all children – the same task might require the teacher to spend more time and effort directing attention to the visual aspects for one child, but to the auditory aspects for another child.

The visual system

We might use the analogy of the eye being like a camera and capturing images that are complete and interpreted. This analogy is too simplistic. The brain has to construct visual meaning and make sense of the images that fall on the back of the eye. Our past experiences are important in helping us see what is around us. We have to learn to see – it is not simply a passive process.

This combining of previous learning and light and dark falling on the retina results in what we 'see'. It involves 'bottom-up processing' in which single points of light are gradually built up into more and more complex shapes and objects. It also involves 'top-down processing' in which the brain uses what it expects to see to make sense of the visual information that is being received. The end result is that shapes and images emerge out of complex (and sometimes incomplete) visual information. Optical illusions and visual pastimes such as stereograms help us experience at first hand the complexities and marvels of visual perception.

In the context of dyslexia there are several questions that are of concern:

- Can the child actually see the words or do they need glasses to correct visual difficulties?
- Are both eyes able to track together and can the brain combine the image to form a stable shape of the word or letter?
- Can the movement of the eyes between successive images be suppressed so that the image of text appears stable and does not look as if the letters are constantly moving?
- Is sight acute enough for a clear image to be formed on the retina for the size of text presented?
- Can the reader form whole word shapes (gestalts) fluently without having to decode each feature of each letter?
- Can the reader deal adequately with different colour and different levels of contrast?
- How well can the reader perceive spatial relationships and manipulate shape and orientation in their mind?

Many of these questions can be answered by a thorough eye-test carried out by an ophthalmologist.

Binocular stability

Each eye is controlled by muscles attached to the eye ball and can move independently. As a child develops they learn to adjust the position of each eye so that they both look at the object being viewed. An object that is a long way from the face will require less of an angle than an object close to the face. The brain uses the angle between the eyes to help judge distance.

In some children the muscles in one eye may be better developed than those in the other and the eye can turn more effectively (the other eye is sometimes referred to as a 'lazy eye'). Sometimes the weakness in eye-muscles is sufficient to be noticeable when looking at the child – this leads to a 'squint' (medical name: strabismus).

Squints can be managed by patching, spectacles or surgery. The effect of patching (ocular occlusion) on reading has been investigated by John Stein (1994). He found that children with stable binocular control could read on average 6.3 months better at the end of each of the first three years of primary school than those with poor binocular control (Stein, 1996). It could be argued that the development of reading skill leads to greater binocular control as muscle control develops through greater exposure to the reading task. Indeed, Stein (1996) reports development of ocular stability through maturation when tested using the Dunlop Test[1] (see the table).

---

[1] The Dunlop test is a test of ocular stability in which the child views a post next to a door through a stereoscope or synotophore. The child starts with a fused image and then slowly moves the tubes apart. One image of the post will appear to move towards the door and the child is asked which one. This is repeated 10 times. If it is always the same image that moves then the child has a fixed reference. If there is a mixed response (more than 2/10), then the child has an unfixed reference and unstable binocular control.

Age of child	% with ocular stability
6 years old	54
7 years old	70
9 years old	85

However, Stein has found that when younger readers are matched for reading age with older poor readers, the younger readers have better binocular control. Attempts to correct this defect using ocular occlusion of the left eye for six months have led to substantial improvements in reading ability in 51% of the children in Stein's study (Stein, 1996; Stein *et al.*, 2000) and similar improvements have been reported by Rennie (1996). On average reading gains of 20.6 months were made in one year. It has been shown that a short period of monocular occlusion can lead to children overcoming their binocular visual confusion permanently, possibly by allowing one eye to learn to control its own direction (Stein *et al.*, 2000).

Condition	Reading age in months			
	Start	3 months	6 months	9 months
Not occluded	81.3	86.1	89.1	93.0
Occluded	82.9	92.5	94.3	97.7

The results of Stein *et al.* (2000) are shown in the second table. It can be seen the greatest overall gain in reading age was for pupils who received the occlusion treatment, with most of the increase occurring in the first three months.

Saccades

When reading the eye can focus on a small amount of the text in one go consisting of approximately five letters ahead and three letters behind the current tracking position. It has to flick along the line of text to see what comes next in a series of saccades. Each flick takes about 30ms and the fixations last longer 250ms (Stein and Talcott, 1999).

It is thought that the magnocellular system is responsible for controlling saccadic movements and therefore a dysfunctional magnocellular system would lead to difficulties in achieving a stable image of text for reading. We are unaware of the saccadic movements because visual processing is inhibited between movements and prevents us from seeing the blur of visual images that must fall upon the retina at this time. The mechanisms responsible for this must respond to two images, one from each eye, in order for us to adequately control and co-ordinate the saccadic movements of both eyes to achieve a consistently overlapping visual image. Failure to achieve a stable binocular control may result in images appearing to move or change position (mild oscillopsia).

Oscillopsia makes the world appear to be in continuous motion as the small involuntary movements of the eye give rise to the apparent motion of objects in the real world and leads to the words on the page appearing to move around (Stein, 1996). This must be particularly difficult for a child who has reached the phonics stage of reading and needs to link a sound to a small stable image of a letter.

Stein (1996) has carried out a number of studies to compare dyslexic children with normal readers and has shown:

- They have lower fixation stability when trying to focus on a small object.
- Unstable binocular control leads to more visual errors when reading non-words.
- Error rates are decreased if print size is increased.
- EEG measurements of activity in the magnocellular region are reduced and abnormal when visual stimuli of low spatial frequency and low contrast are presented.

Interestingly, it seems that the signals reaching the magnocelluar layer can be moderated through the use of coloured light. A red background light has been found to attenuate the response of the transient channels in primates. Dyslexics have been found to comprehend text better when it is presented in a blue light compared with either red or white light (Lovegrove, 1994; Lovegrove and Williams, 1993; Williams, 1999). Williams (1999) claims that manipulating characteristics of the physical stimulus can compensate for deficits in the magnocellular system and lead to improvements for up to 80% of dyslexics. This is the basis for Irlem Lenses and Irlem Filters.

Gestalts

Pandemonium theory (Selfridge, 1959) argued for layers of cells that would respond with increasing intensity the more closely a stimulus matched their template. As they respond they pass information to the next layer of cells that have a more complex template. We might imagine that this continues until every word has a visual template. If this was the case then reading would simply require a whole word recognition for meaning to be extracted.

One difficulty with this theory is that experienced readers are able to recognize letters and words even when they are in a different orientation or written in a different font. A second difficulty is that the same features make different letters when the orientation changes (hence the saying – mind your 'p's and 'q's). This suggests that reading is more than simply decoding features.

The gestaltist view is that visual perception is something more than just a pattern of light and dark (the whole is greater than the sum of the constituent parts). The ability to see a whole shape from the features that make it up means that the perceptual system does not have to work too hard at decoding visual input. While this makes visual perception faster it does sometimes lead to inaccuracies and we see what we expect to see. Some visual illusions make use of this. In the example shown, the same visual features can be interpreted in more than one way:

This suggests that prediction and meaning have a role to play in reading. The reader is able to guess what the next word might be without actually seeing it. Visual perception then confirms the guess. The rules of language and what has already been decoded are suffi-cient to play 'the psycholinguistic guessing game'.

Colour and contrast

Colour blindness is more common in boys than girls. Typically two colours are seen as the same (red and green or blue and yellow). A few people cannot see colour at all and view the world in monochromatic shades of grey. Some people find that they can see one colour more easily than others.

Contrast refers to the difference between light and dark parts of the image. The more contrast there is the more the different parts of the image are distinguishable from each other. Some colours of pens and chalk do not provide good contrast when used on boards and this may make reading more difficult.

Contrast and colour are important when thinking about the adaptive learning environment. They are relevant to:

- handouts
- textbooks
- board work
- use of monitors and screens.

It is also important to think about how the quality of the image may decrease in a room with poor lighting or where reflections are apparent.

The auditory and phonological system

Hearing relies on vibrations in the air passing through clear air passages to an intact membrane that transmits vibration to three tiny bones. In turn these pass the vibrations to the cochlea which contains tiny hairs (cilia) that vibrate with different frequencies. This allows the vibration to be turned into a nerve signal that can then be processed by the brain. Perception and processing of the sound involves more than just detecting it. Awareness of the components of speech (phonemes) is required along with other features of language production and reception.

Difficulties in detecting sound

Mechanical difficulties can arise in any part of the system that takes sound from outside the ear to the point where it is changed into a nerve signal. This can include:

- Perforated ear drum.
- Blocked eustachian tube that prevents the middle ear pressure from equalizing with the external air pressure. This is sometimes referred to as 'glue ear'.
- Damage to the bones or ligaments in the middle ear.
- Damage to the cilia in the cochlea. This means that some frequencies of sound will not be heard as well as other frequencies of sound.

The first three difficulties will result in a child who can hear loud sounds but not soft sounds. A hearing test can identify the degree of global loss. For example, glue ear may result in a 30 decibel (dB) loss of hearing, if a child has a cold. As the cold clears up so may the glue ear. This may mean that hearing comes and goes and this provides inconsistent learning opportunities. Other children may have a more permanent hearing loss that requires an aid.

When some frequencies are lost, the child is able to hear the sounds of some letters or to hear particular phonemes better than others. Fricatives tend to be high-frequency sounds, vowels tend to be low-frequency sounds.

	Sounds likely to be missing from normally spoken words
30 dB loss	Z, x, p, h, f, th, s
50 dB loss	All except for e, l, u
High-frequency loss >4 kHz	K, f, th, s
Low-frequency loss <500 Hz	Z, v, j, m, n, d, e

Phonological awareness

The sounds heard in speech are referred to as phonemes. English language has between 44 and 46 phonemes, depending on dialect.

Phonological awareness refers to our ability to hear these phonemes and to manipulate them:

- blending phonemes, e.g. adding 'sp' to 'lash' to make 'splash';
- splitting phonemes, e.g. deleting 'tr' from 'truck' to make 'uck';
- Spoonerisms, e.g. '**Work** is the curse of the **drink**ing classes'; 'You've **h**issed my **m**ystery lectures';
- noticing onsets and alliterations;
- noticing rhymes;
- rapidly naming words;
- repeating unfamiliar words, long polysyllabic words or pseudowords.

The ability to do these types of things is essentially a linguistic skill and does not rely on reading. However, it is necessary for reading and reading helps with phonological development.

The kinaesthetic system

As we use our muscles we develop a memory for our body shape (our body image) and we are aware of the position of different parts of our body. This is referred to as muscle memory and the detection of extension or relaxation in muscles is called proprioception.

At first movements require a lot of effort as we try to control where our limbs are. After a while though, we can carry out quite complex movements (such as driving a car) automatically. It can take many repetitions of a movement under conscious control before it becomes automatic (some estimate as many as 2,500 times). Teaching pupils to write in a cursive script is believed to encourage a motor memory for how a word is written. For some dyslexic children the process does not become automatic and this means that movement remains under conscious control and requires constant effort. This will affect handwriting but it can also affect the pupil's ability to recognize when a spelling 'feels right'.

During adolescence there is a growth spurt. The rate of growth of limbs can exceed the brain's ability to adapt and form a new body image. This can result in some clumsiness – this is temporary and normal control is restored when the body image catches up with the actual body size.

As infants develop they go through a phase when many brain cells are destroyed. This is a normal part of maturation and results in the most efficient neural pathways remaining. For some children this reduction in brain cells does not always happen. Many more pathways remain and the brain has to make decisions about which pathways to use. This can lead to less efficient pathways being used and results in a slowness of speed and reaction time. It can also lead to clumsiness of movement or clumsiness in organizing ideas (referred to as dyspraxia).

Children with these kinds of difficulties generally need longer to complete tasks and can be supported through:

- using writing frames to support organization of ideas;
- teaching mind-maps to aid planning;
- using larger pencils to lighten the grip and effort needed when making writing movements;
- providing wider lines so that changes of direction do not need to be so tight;
- high resistance writing materials, which provide more feedback and strengthen information about where muscles are.

Positive traits in dyslexia

Dyslexia is a condition that generally leads to people thinking about limitations and the way the condition stops children from accessing the curriculum or recording their ideas. This way of framing dyslexia can be damaging to children – it wears away their self-esteem and always focuses on their shortcomings.

However, having dyslexia can enable some young people to develop amazing talents. This may be because they are able to process certain types of information more effectively, or it may be because they develop compensatory strategies.

An example of a compensatory strategy found in some dyslexics is a very good verbal memory. This comes about because teachers normally support children during class discussions by writing information on the board. If you are dyslexic and cannot read the information easily, then you have no choice but to remember it. This seems to develop memory skills for verbal information.

One strength reported by many dyslexics is increased artistic ability. Perhaps because they are less able to communicate verbally or in writing, some dyslexics develop their artistic skills as a means of expressing themselves.

Teachers and parents can help dyslexic children search for their talents and strengths and encourage them to develop those areas of interest at which they do well.

Famous people who are thought to have been dyslexic are often cited in newspapers, examples from The *Guardian* (1998) include:

- Leonardo da Vinci

- Hans Christian Andersen

- Auguste Rodin

- Thomas Edison

- Winston Churchill

- Albert Einstein

- Richard Rogers

- Tom Cruise

Whether some of the earlier people in the list would be defined as dyslexic by today's standards remains unclear. But the message is important – dyslexic difficulties should not be a barrier to doing great things.

The challenge for teachers

Learning and teaching are reciprocal and occur as a social inter-action in which the more competent teacher structures the learning environment and tasks of the less competent pupil. This reframing of teaching and learning means that often children's learning diffi-culties are seen as teachers' teaching difficulties. Teaching is viewed as involving more than *delivering* a curriculum; what requires some thought is how the teacher can help the learner to access the curriculum and record ideas.

The model of intervention changes from attempting to improve children's performance through remedial teaching, to inviting the teacher to engage in a reflection of their teaching strategies. How will the teacher respond to the child's needs while covering the breadth of content of the curriculum? How can challenging work be presented to a bright child who has difficulty accessing text or recording their ideas in writing?

Schools are expected to include dyslexic pupils in the mainstream of classroom activities. This means that teachers will need to notice differences in pupil performance and respond to them. They will need to know what to look for and to have a range of strategies that allow effective responses. Effective support can be provided without having to resort to Statements of SEN, but may involve LEA support agencies and the efficient deployment of LEA resources.

Individual education plans continue to focus on remedial education with clearly defined Specific, Measurable, Achievable, Relevant, Timed (SMART) targets. Good programmes are those that are provided on a Daily basis and are Structured, Cumulative and Multi-sensory (D-SCuM). There are plenty of packages available to help teachers address remediation. What is often missing is a statement on the IEP about how the child will be supported through the adaptation of the learning environment or teaching strategies used.

Perhaps IEPs need to be widened in their scope to include specific classroom management and support techniques. This would then prompt class teachers and subject teachers when thinking about planning their lessons. It could also prompt parents into thinking about things they could do to help their child during the day and with homework. (See pages 131–140.)

The next chapter invites you to think about how children with reading and spelling difficulties can be supported on a day-to-day basis in the classroom, doing their normal work and being included in the mainstream curriculum. The case studies on pages 24 and 25 exemplify some of these children.

Summary

- There are many different definitions of dyslexia – each emphasizes something slightly different. This can make the term dyslexia seem unsuitable as a diagnostic term. However, all agree that the term implies a significant difficulty in reading and spelling.
- Some definitions acknowledge that dyslexia is a much wider problem that interferes with other areas of life as well as learning in school. What is certain is that no two dyslexic children are the same – each has slightly different presenting difficulties. Each child also has a different range of strengths that can be developed.
- Somehow, teachers and parents have to notice these difficulties and respond to them. This book explores some of the solutions that can be tried.

Five case studies

Charles

Charles attends his local secondary school. When there are class discussions, he seems bright – always keen to answer the teacher's questions and he has lots of ideas.

At parents' evenings his teachers often comment on the extent of his general knowledge – but also on his lack of ability to 'get anything down on paper'. Homework is never done; he never has the right equipment for lessons. When he does manage to produce something it is untidy, poorly set out and his ideas are poorly structured. His spelling is described as 'weird' and he takes an age to read though questions. His test results in class do not reflect what he can do. Some teachers think he is lazy.

John

John is a Year 5 pupil – he's in trouble again. Every lesson his teacher has to tell him to stop wandering around and to sit in his place! As soon as the class starts work he's off – chatting to this one, borrowing a rubber off that one – or just sharpening his pencil. He must get though several pencils in a week!

Ahmed

Ahmed is superb at art – his drawing of the school is up on the wall in the headteacher's office and some of his collage work was displayed in the library. He is popular with his peers and was chosen to be the captain of the school football team.

His literacy is not so good. In his Key Stage 2 SATs he managed to get Level 2 overall for English, while in mathematics he achieved a Level 5.

Julie

Julie is 8 years old. She has a history of ear infections and 'glue ear'. Her speech is unclear and indistinct with sounds mixed up. She has seen a Speech and Language Therapist and things are improving.

In school, her reading is well behind the rest of the class. Her knowledge of letter sounds is incomplete. She gets upset because her reading book is not the same as everyone else's. At home, reading is a real battle – tears and tantrums are common.

Callum

Callum's mum is worried. Despite his poor reading and writing, he has done well in his primary school. This has been because his teacher knows him well and has been very supportive. But in September, he will transfer to the High School. 'What will happen to him then? He won't be able to keep up with the work and he will get lost in such a big school.'

I wonder how he'll cope?

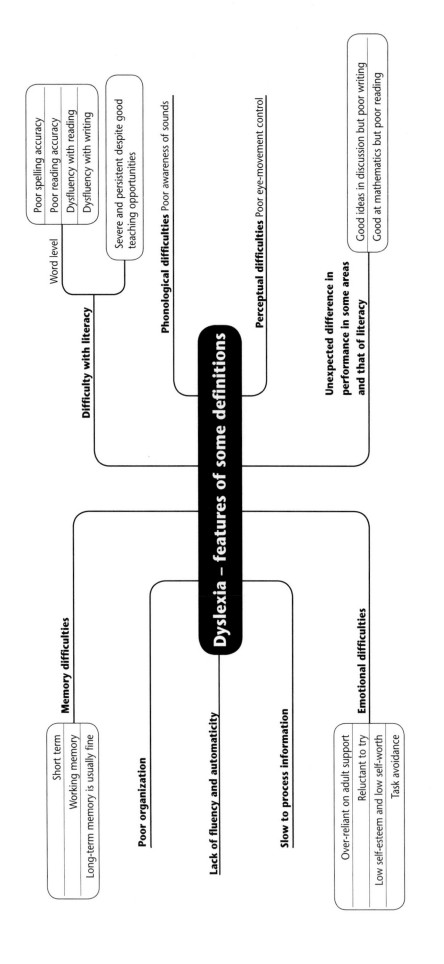

Dyslexia – features of some definitions

Difficulty with literacy

Word level
- Poor spelling accuracy
- Poor reading accuracy
- Dysfluency with reading
- Dysfluency with writing

Severe and persistent despite good teaching opportunities

Phonological difficulties Poor awareness of sounds

Perceptual difficulties Poor eye-movement control

Unexpected difference in performance in some areas and that of literacy
- Good ideas in discussion but poor writing
- Good at mathematics but poor reading

Memory difficulties
- Short term
- Working memory
- Long-term memory is usually fine

Poor organization

Lack of fluency and automaticity

Slow to process information

Emotional difficulties
- Over-reliant on adult support
- Reluctant to try
- Low self-esteem and low self-worth
- Task avoidance

2 | Identifying Strengths and Weaknesses

It is all too easy to emphasize the negative aspects of dyslexia and unwittingly contribute to a child's feelings of inadequacy and failure. While assessing strengths and weaknesses can be useful – for pupil, parents and teachers – it is important to remember to 'accentuate the positive' at all times and remind pupils of what they CAN do as well as identifying and addressing the tasks that present difficulties for them.

A good starting place to protect children's self-esteem is to list all the things they do well. This can be done using notes, key words, drawings or photographs. Celebration charts, merit points and certificates can be used judiciously to reward effort and boost self-confidence.

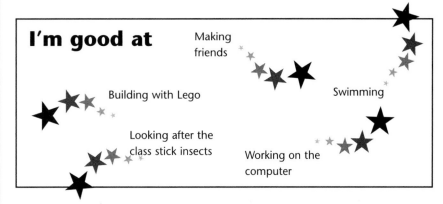

A great deal of celebration in schools is to do with neat presentation of work, well-written text and expressive reading aloud. But there are many other attributes/skills/actions worthy of recognition:

- being polite/kind/thoughtful/helpful/patient/persistent;
- being good at art, music, model-making, cookery, sport;
- keeping a secret, remembering something, taking care of animals, befriending 'the new boy'.

Checklist

The different definitions of dyslexia suggest points that could be included on a checklist. When completing the list, remember that children are developing all the time and think about how well a particular pupil compares with others of the same age. This is important since a child aged 18 months would show all of the signs of dyslexia on the DfEE checklist for primary school teachers (DfEE, undated).

The checklist is constructed from the main definitions and phrased in a positive way so that you can think about what the child *can* do. Several columns have been added so that you can record progress over time.

Name: Date of birth:	Rating scale **Blank** = can't do yet **1** = can do with help **2** = can do independently **3** = can do well			
Date:				
Speed of processing				
Speaks quickly and fluently				
Reads quickly				
Writes quickly				
Solves problems quickly				
Memory				
Remembers three things when told to bring them from another room				
Remembers a telephone number				
Can relate events that have happened days ago				
Remembers to do things that are planned				
Retains new knowledge				
Can recall address				
Retains new words that are read				
Retains new spellings				
Independence				
Ties shoelaces				
Dresses self				
Reading				
Can tell if two words sound the same (rhyme)				
Recognizes all of the letter sounds or names				
Can sort out similar looking letters (e.g. 'b' from 'd', 'u' from 'n')				
Has strategies for attempting new words				
Manages to read the small linking words (e.g. a, and, the, of, it, is)				
Can keep track of place and position when reading				

Writing				
Writes name unaided				
Writes numbers in correct orientation				
Makes own notes following discussion				
Writes with few crossings out				
Writes in a cursive style				
Spelling				
Spells words consistently				
Spellings make sense				
Can recognize when an error has been made				
85% or more of spellings are correct				
Co-ordination				
Rides a bike				
Has a clear preference or handedness				
Knows which is right and left				
Produces well-formed letters				
Is able to produce clear drawings				
Holds pencil correctly				
Organization				
Sets out written work well				
Has an even space at the start of each line next to the margin or page edge				
Remembers to bring pencil case, books, PE kit to school				
Behaviour				
Is able to sit still and concentrate on non-literacy tasks				
Is able to sit still and concentrate on literacy tasks				
Chooses to read				
Chooses to write				
Participates in all aspects of lesson				
Keen to go to school				
Keen to go to lessons				

Reading and spelling ages

There will be a range of reading abilities and spelling abilities within any classroom just as there will be a range of heights and weights. To some extent, reading and spelling achievement as measured by tests will depend upon the particular test used. Such assessments can be useful however, especially when shared with all staff who come into contact with a dyslexic pupil, as a way of reminding them of his limitations. If teachers know that a pupil has a reading age of 7.0 in his first year of secondary school, they will realize that he is going to need a lot of support in using a textbook that requires a reading age of 11.0. There are instances, however, where detailed testing is carried out by the SENCo and support staff, as a means of gathering diagnostic information and monitoring individual progress, but outcomes are not shared with subject teachers.

Reading and spelling ages of children considered in the average range for reading

Different reading and spelling tests give different age scores for the same child. Most people consider that an average child would have a reading and spelling age equal to their chronological age and worry if the test shows that they are below this level. However, there is a spread around 'the average' with the normal distribution curve showing that most children have a reading and spelling age either just below or above their chronological age.

If children's test scores are put in order so they go from the lowest to the highest, then the child's rank order position can be obtained. This goes from 1 to 100, and is referred to as a centile score. Statistically, the average is considered to go from the 16th centile position to the 84th centile position.

The table below shows the ages obtained on three common tests used by psychologists to measure reading. They show the age of children who are performing at the 16th centile level (i.e. at the bottom end of the 'average' band). The Code of Practice for Special Educational Needs suggests that remediation is only necessary if a child is not making adequate progress and is falling below the majority of their peers. The spread in ability gets wider as children get older. Being just over one year behind is seen as a cause for concern at age 7, but by the age of 16 a pupil would be three to four years behind before attracting the same concern.

Age of child	BAS-II	WORD	NARA-II
5.0–6.0 is below the minimum age measurable on the test selected.			
7.0	5.9 to 5.10	6.3	6.1
8.0	6.10	7.0	6.7
9.0	7.10	7.9	7.3
10.0	8.3	8.9	7.10
11.0	8.9 to 8.10	8.9	8.6
12.0	9.10 to 9.11	9.3	9.1
13.0	10.10 to 10.11	9.6	9.6
14.0	11.5 to 11.7	10.3	Not suitable for children over 12.11
15.0	12.5 to 12.8	10.9	
16.0	13.6 to 13.8	11.9	

Classroom observations

The Code of Practice for Special Educational Needs places an emphasis on teachers noticing children's difficulties and then adjusting their teaching accordingly. This means that teachers need to be on the lookout for potential difficulties that the dyslexic child might have and then respond with a suitable strategy to ameliorate the difficulties.

The kinds of questions that might be helpful are:

- What am I asking the pupils to do?
- What parts of this task can this particular pupil do without any help?
- What might they be able to do if they work with a more competent peer?
- What could they do in a different way?
- How have they done similar things before?
- How might I be able to break the task down so that they can achieve success using added structure?
- Where might an adult be needed to help them? In what way?

Chapter 3, Classroom Settings and Supportive Strategies, provides a long list of suggestions for helping dyslexic children.

Noting things that help

Dyslexia has been found to 'run in families'. Often, if a child is diagnosed as dyslexic, then one of their parents or grandparents also had difficulty with learning to read or spell. This provides a useful way of finding things that might work with the child. Ask the adult questions such as: 'What helped you?', 'How did you solve such and such a problem?', 'How do you …?'

Parents can take time to note what seems to help at home. Equally, when a child is going to transfer to a new class, the existing teacher can make a note of things that have helped.

Analysing spelling patterns

Some checklists include the item 'bizarre spelling' and we often consider some children's spelling as being very idiosyncratic. It seems to make sense to them but is not accepted in English. However, an understanding of how spelling skills develop allows us to look beyond this framing.

As children's spelling skills start to emerge they start to encounter different strategies that they can use to help them to express their thoughts in writing. Some of these strategies are explicitly taught and this means that some types of mistakes are predictable for children of a given age. As children learn new strategies, their attempts become more and more like the target word. Some children do not progress in their learning of new spelling strategies as fast as their peers. This means that they continue to use immature or inefficient strategies. Some children do not learn some strategies as well as others and this reflects their strengths and weaknesses in spelling. Understanding these strengths and weaknesses or the range of strategies that the child is able to use will help us to decide the kinds of approaches to use in remediation or the features of particular spellings to emphasize during classwork.

There are two ways for the teacher to help a child who is not spelling as well as other children in the class. The first is to look at the spellings carefully and see whether there are some clues to the strengths and weaknesses that the child may have. The second is to look at the types of strategies that the child uses when trying to spell a word.

1. Looking for verbal and visual strategies

Somehow children need to learn that particular letters can represent specific sounds in words. In some languages this is easier than others because the languages are transparent and the letters only have one sound. In the kinds of words that young children use, this is also mostly the case in English (about 85% of words are estimated as being phonologically regular). There has to be a linking of sound (phonemes) with shapes of letters (graphemes). Treiman (1997) presented a model of spelling development that focused on the phonological development of spelling. In her paper she described dyslexic spelling as being qualitatively similar to that produced by younger children. An analysis of the types of visual errors that children make based on how the perceptual system works was described by Squires (2003). The two types of errors are evident when children start to learn that each letter contributes to particular sounds in written words (the grapheme-phoneme stage of development).

Verbal errors made at the phoneme-grapheme stage

- *Phonemic representation* – there is increasing consistency of letter use to represent the sounds that the child hears, e.g. 'eat' is written as 'it' (i/t).
- *Consonant omission* – the child has difficulties when the sound is represented by more than one letter. Typical errors include 'drik' for 'drink', 'cod' for 'cold' or 'wom' for 'warm'.
- *Vowel omission* – the vowels are not needed to write the sounds in words and are sometimes missed out, e.g. 'hotl' for 'hotel', 'hr' for 'her'.
- *Immature speech patterns are evident in spelling* – examples include saying 'jr' instead of 'dr' (e.g. 'jragon') or 'ch' instead of 'tr'.
- *Phonologically plausible but orthographic errors* – particular letter

reversals are more likely than others because children remember what the sound is.

Visual-spatial errors made at the phoneme-grapheme stage

- *Sequence errors* – the letters are present but in the wrong order, e.g. 'wtiring'.
- *Addition of extra letters* – extra letters are added to the word, e.g. 'offten'.
- *Omission of letters* – letters are left out, e.g. 'stiker'.
- *Orientation of letters* – letters are confused with similar looking letters, e.g. u/n, w/m, b/d/p/q.
- *Form* – confusions are related to the form of the letter, e.g. n/h, i/j, i/l, a/e/o. This includes gestalt errors, for example perceiving closure on 'i' to make 'l' or on 'c' to make 'o'.
- *Global errors* – the word has the right start and right end and is about the right length.

The subcategories of error described above help us to understand what type of processing the child might be relying on or what types of processing the child might have difficulty with. A simple recording table will help to place the types of errors that children make. Some errors could be classified as either visual or verbal. This means that the same word might appear on both sides.

Interpreting the pattern of scores

We can use the pattern of scores to help us understand whether the child might have a weakness in either verbal-phonological or visual-spatial processing. This could allow us to explore this hypothesis further, e.g. by asking for hearing or sight checks or by conducting an assessment of phonological skills.

We need to take a sample of the child's free writing and start to identify errors and decide what type of mistakes the child could be making. Sometimes we are not entirely sure and the child's mistake may be put into more than one category. This is OK at this stage – we are not able to look inside the child's head to see how the word was processed, we can only gain an insight by interpreting the clues in the writing.

In the table overleaf, we have identified errors according to which information processing system might be responsible for the error. Most of the errors identify a weakness, *except phonologically plausible*. The PP errors are telling us that the child is over-reliant on the sound of the word and is not paying attention to the shape of the word. This means that the child is very good at using the sound of the letters and the word to approximate the spelling of the word.

Verbal score is the total of errors made in the first four categories – the

Target word and child's attempt	Possible verbal error Phonemic, Consonant, Vowel, Immature, PP Phonologically Plausible					Possible visual error Sequence, Addition (+), Omission (−), Orientation, Form, Global					
	P	C	V	I	PP	S	+	−	O	F	G
Totals *Each row only counts once in each category*	**Verbal =** P+C+V+I−**PP**					**Visual =**					

PP score. Visual-spatial score is the total of errors made in the last six categories

For this to work effectively we may have attributed an error to more than one category – if this is the case we can only count it **once**. We should end up with a score for visual and verbal errors – if one is higher than the other then it represents a relative weakness and we can use this to guide our teaching.

A worked example

Analysis in practice

In real life, children do not make just one type of mistake. Here are two examples of spelling from Andrew, an 8-year-old boy diagnosed with mild dyslexia.

Sample A

Home alown tow is about a boy who is supostoo go to a place in Spane but he [went] to New Yorck. When he notesers [he] go's and check's in at a hotell with his dads credickard.

Sample B

This year I had to days for my birthday. On satarday I went to cricket for an hour then I came back home and got redey for my party what was Laser Quest. We had twety minits and then we had a brake then we had a other 20 minits. there wore some big gise who ganged up on [us] after that we ad some Mck donels I whent home and played abit. Then we had some lovly cory after that we woched rokey 2. I was very tierd after that. In the morning it was father's day and my birthday I got lots of presents nice one's to. At 2 o'clock my famerly came and I got some more precents I played with my precents then we went in and looked at some micters of Astrayleaer because my anty had been there. After that they all left and I played with my car set then I went up sters and played on my new game then I went to bed.

Sample A has been done for you (overleaf). Sample B is given for you to practise with.

Target word and child's attempt	Possible verbal error **P**honemic, **C**onsonant, **V**owel, **I**mmature, **PP** Phonologically Plausible					Possible visual error **S**equence, Addition (+), Omission (−), **O**rientation, **F**orm, **G**lobal					
	P	**C**	**V**	**I**	**PP**	**S**	**+**	**−**	**O**	**F**	**G**
Alone alown					✓						
Two tow						✓					
Supposed supostoo					✓						
Spain Spane					✓						
York Yorck					✓		✓				
Notices notesers					✓						
Goes go's								✓			
Hotel hotell					✓		✓				
Credit card credickard					✓						
Totals ***Each row only counts once in each category***	**Verbal = −7** P+C+V+I−**PP**					**Visual = 4**					

In this particular case we can conclude that Andrew seems to be over-reliant on the verbal representation of the word and has good phonological skills. Most errors are phonologically plausible. Visual errors suggest that he is not attending to how the word looks. Our remediation might try to emphasize how the word looks or we might teach spelling rules that explain how the same sound can be represented in different ways (e.g. using THRASS).

2. Looking at the strategies the child is able to use

Children's ability to spell changes qualitatively as they get older. This development occurs partly through structured teaching and partly through exposure to richer and more complex text.

A broad model of development shows spelling moving through rough stages.

Pre-spelling

Early spellings start off as being simple representations of words – scribblings that are recognizable as being different from the child's drawings. Perhaps the marks are smaller or they travel in a line. The child is playing at writing and perhaps copying what parents or older siblings seem to be doing. Big objects tend to get big words.

Syllabic-grapheme

By reception stage, children are starting to learn that letters convey meaning. At this stage they may expect a single letter to represent a syllable.

Grapheme-phoneme correspondence

At this level, children learn that letters make particular sounds and these can be modified by the sounds around them. Common errors have been covered above.

Morphemic spelling

The child starts to take account of meaning and etymology. For example 'heal' and 'health' both carry the same meaning and have the same morpheme 'heal'. Errors now involve selecting the wrong morpheme.

Some spellings cannot be easily assigned to just one category and may need to be placed in more than one category. But a diagnostic count can be made of the types of errors made and this can guide the next step in remediation.

In order to see where a child is up to we can map their spellings in much the same way as we did for visual or verbal errors. This would give us an idea of what strategy we need to teach next.

This table allows a sample of the child's writing to be recorded and the teacher can then make a judgement about which developmental level has been reached. Several samples can be considered before deciding where the child is up to.

Examples of child's spelling	Pre-spelling	Syllabic-grapheme	Grapheme-phoneme	Morphemic

Remedial programmes

For pupils with significant problems, part of a school's response is often the instigation of some sort of structured remedial programme. This can be an opportunity to focus on specific areas of difficulty, often outside the normal classroom situation and away from the attentions of curious peers.

For children with difficulties severe enough to require a Statement of Special Educational Needs it has been found that:

- progress is better when children's needs are identified early and Statements carry specialist support;
- better progress is made when additional focused teaching is provided;
- good progress in reading is linked to a highly structured programme of teaching often involving a multi-sensory approach (a recommendation was made that this should be available earlier on and before a Statement was required);

- effective programmes go beyond merely hearing the child read and include teaching the use of context cues; discussion of the content to aid understanding; systematic teaching of word groups and the sounds of clusters of letters.
(Ofsted,1999)

These features can be applied equally, of course, to pupils who are receiving additional support at the *School Action* or *School Action Plus* stage.

A feature of many good remedial programmes is repetition and over-learning of materials that the child finds difficult to learn. Well-designed programmes involve daily practice often lasting only 10 to 15 minutes. This is because memory is more efficient when practice is distributed across several learning periods rather than massed into one learning session. It has other important gains too:

- The child expects the learning to take place; the routine helps to prepare him for the activity.
- The activities tend to be fast-paced and this reduces the opportunities for attention wandering and concentration waning.
- Short duration tasks are easier to fit into the busy schedule of a school or the domestic demands placed upon a busy parent.

Precision teaching is a good example of distributed practice and may include exercises such as a one-minute daily exercise to see how many 'b's and 'd's the child can successfully read from a grid of randomly presented 'b's and 'd's. This type of exercise provides the child with instant feedback and always focuses on success. Progress can be easily monitored by keeping a daily count or by using a weekly probe sheet.

Learning stages

Learning progresses through well-defined stages:

1. *Unknown skills and knowledge* – learning has not taken place.
2. *Acquisition* – the child is just starting to learn, getting it right on some days but not others.
3. *Mastery learning* – the child gets it right all the time in the learning situation, but does not apply the new knowledge consistently in the classroom.
4. *Generalization* – the child gets it right all the time, in the learning situation and beyond.

Sometimes children fail in teaching programmes because the pace of the programme is too quick and is focused on the teaching materials rather than the child's learning. The materials move on to the next skill or item of knowledge while the child is left at the acquisition stage. Without consolidation they will not master the skill or knowledge and will not be able to apply it in their everyday work. This is sometimes compounded when programmes are designed in which each piece of new learning builds upon learning that is expected to have taken place in earlier parts of the programme.

Sometimes a child seems to have learnt a word and then after a couple of days they can no longer read or spell it. It is as if the word has not been retained. However, it is more likely that the child is still acquiring the word. How do we know that the child has mastered the words that they have been learning? We can record learning and measure how many presentations it takes to get the words right consistently (this is referred to as 100% learning). For instance we might ask the child to learn to read four words presented randomly on a daily basis. We might notice that some days the child gets the word and other days they do not. We could decide to count 100% learning as the point where the child has got the word right correctly for six presentations.

Word											
The	✓		✓	✓			✓	✓	✓	✓	✓
Here	✓	✓	✓	✓	✓	✓					
Where		✓	✓			✓	✓			✓	✓
There							✓	✓			✓
These											
Which											
While											

In this example, we can see that the teacher has identified some words that she would like the child to learn. For the first few days, he has been learning three words (the, here and where). The word 'the' is being acquired for the first six days and then is correctly identified. Better discrimination is made for 'here' and the word is considered mastered after Day 6. On Day 7, 'here' is then replaced with a new word ('there'), so that the child still has three words to learn. The word 'where' is proving more problematic and seems to be retained for only a couple of days at a time. For some children, some words remain problematic but will be acquired eventually – I have known some children have 40 or more learning episodes before the word is mastered. It takes a little longer to ensure that the child transfers the skill practised during remediation so that the word is generalized to normal reading and writing.

Good programmes need to take into account the fact that memory fades and needs renewal of the 'memory trace' to sustain learning. Some teaching assistants ask the child to recall one thing he has

Computer programs from CALSC have been used successfully in some schools. Mastering Memory is a general program for children to identify their strengths and to help them develop strategies for memorizing information (www.calsc.co.uk). Some children seem to know what works for them and have good methods in place; others need direct teaching if they are to learn how to learn.

learned at the end of each lesson and ask the same question at the beginning of the next lesson. This reinforces recall and, by saying it out loud, it helps to fix the idea in the mind. Some intervention programmes incorporate interleaved learning in which old material is interleaved with the new. Once learning has reached generalization level, learning is sustained through daily use and practice. At this level, interleaved learning is not necessary.

When selecting a remedial programme we need to somehow take the child's classroom-based learning into the remedial situation and vice versa. One way of doing this is to start with the mistakes that the child makes with literacy, e.g. using miscue analysis in reading. The teacher could start by looking at the child's writing and doing some targeted marking to find the three most common errors made by the child in spelling. This would then allow remedial teaching to focus on the types of errors made. Progress during remedial work then feeds back into improved accuracy in classwork. Positive feedback about this will increase the child's self-confidence and their view of themselves as a successful independent learner. If the teacher continues to target-mark the words identified earlier then there is feedback about daily performance and a systematic way of monitoring the extent of generalization. Generalization can be further supported by the class teacher looking for opportunities to teach the spelling throughout the day. For example:

- drawing attention to the spelling rule in whole class work;
- checking the child's application of the spelling 'in passing' through the lesson;
- teaching the spelling rule and reminding of the spelling rule through group work or whole class work, or in visiting the child to provide individual support;
- having reminders of the target spelling rules displayed around the room in a variety of formats;
- playing 'spot the mistake' by deliberately making the mistake in board work and then asking the class to spot the mistake and say how the word could be corrected.

Making good links between support workers (teaching assistants, specialist advisory teachers, SENCos) and the class teacher or subject teachers will maximize learning and generalization. For instance if the remedial programme is focusing on breaking words down into syllables as a word-attack strategy when reading, then this can be extended into the classroom:

- When the child gets stuck on a word when reading a class text, the teacher or teaching assistant can take the child through the stages of breaking the word down and then blending the different segments produced. The teacher comes along and asks the child questions to prompt the actions required, rather than simply telling the child what the word is. If the steps are too large

Vygotsky coined the term 'zone of proximal development' (ZPD) to refer to the presentation of a task that is just beyond the child's unaided ability, but not so difficult that they cannot succeed with adult support. The support is usually in the form of structured questions that guide attention to and reflection about the problem, and develop thinking.

then the adult can break the steps down even further. The child is then able to succeed in the strategy with the adult's help and is learning in the *zone of proximal development*. The emphasis is on the child succeeding and this has a positive effect on the child's self-esteem.

- The class teacher can use the strategy to model the process in whole class teaching for dealing with new words or subject-specific words.

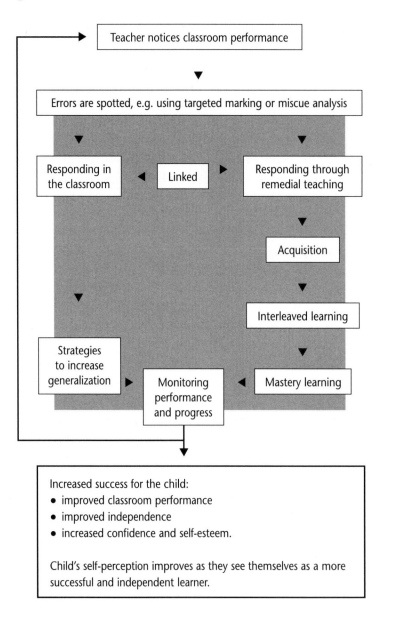

Increased success for the child:
- improved classroom performance
- improved independence
- increased confidence and self-esteem.

Child's self-perception improves as they see themselves as a more successful and independent learner.

Selecting programmes to use with children

There are many published intervention programmes on the market that can be used with children and new programmes are being developed by teachers. The programmes need to be selected so that they match the needs of the child in order the teaching is appropriate. Many contain tests or assessment tools designed to help the teacher decide where to place the child on the programme (*sometimes called placement tests*).

A good remedial programme should be presented on a frequent and regular basis (ideally daily) and in a structured way. It will probably be devised to utilize different senses (sight, sound and touch) and it will build on previous learning. A mnemonic can help us remember these points – D-SCuM (Daily, Structured, Cumulative and Multi-sensory).

A summary of 25 different popular programmes was produced by the DfES. This is an interesting document and provides a good overview of the different intervention programmes. Greg Brooks also introduced a way of comparing the different programmes by looking at the rate of gain made by children (Brooks, 2000). He called this Ratio Gain.

$$\text{Ratio Gain} = \frac{\text{Progress made in months in reading age (or spelling age)}}{\text{Time in months spent on the programme}}$$

An average child is expected to make one month's progress for each month of teaching. The ratio gain would be $1/1 = 1$. This means that if intensive teaching is used to help a child 'catch up' with peers the ratio gain would need to be more than 1. A ratio gain of 2.0 or more was defined as indicating 'good extra progress'.

Adequate progress

When we think about children with literacy difficulties that cannot be accounted for by missed learning opportunities then it seems unrealistic for them to learn at twice the rate of their more able peers. Just how fast should they learn? What would be considered adequate progress? Fortunately, the Code of Practice for Special Educational Needs helps us with different definitions.

The focus is on inclusion. All children are not expected to learn at the same rate, nor are slower learners expected to catch up. There is a suggestion that children will make progress in a way that is adequate for them. The emphasis is on success and not on proving that the child is a failure (Squires, 2004). The term *adequate progress* is used and defined in a variety of ways (Code of Practice p. 68). Each definition has its own implications and these are explored below.

The first definition used seems familiar and has a 'common sense' interpretation about it:

- The pupil 'closes the gap' between their level of attainment and that of their peers. This is a more traditional view and consistent with the idea of catching up or becoming more average rather than remaining below average. This is the definition being encouraged by the Wave 2 and Wave 3 documents for National Literacy and has an expectation that ratio gains will be 2.0 or more.

However, if we are to have a more inclusive education then we need to acknowledge that not all children can be average. Some children will not 'catch up' no matter what we do. They will always learn at a slower rate, even if taught individually and with the best teachers. The Code of Practice recognizes this and offers further definitions.

The following examples show the difficulty of using the definitions meaningfully:

- The attainment gap does not get any wider. This is a difficult definition to interpret. In the simple example of using reading ages to measure children's ability we are faced with the difficulty that a reading age is usually defined as the level that 50% of children achieve on a test at any given age. This means that 50% do not achieve that level and there will be a spread of abilities. As children get older the spread will become wider. This means that a child making normal progress and being classed as an average reader will find that the gap between their age and the reading age expected for children of their chronological age on a particular test will get wider. This leads to other questions about this definition:
  - Does this mean a first centile child remains at the first centile and does not drop to 0.5 centile?
  - Does it mean that the child who is two years behind does not become three years behind?

One way of dealing with this is to consider the intervention being used. We would expect progress to be faster when appropriate teaching is provided. We can modify the formula provided by Brooks to take this into account.

We need to identify the effectiveness of the intervention by comparing progress during the intervention to the progress that would be predicted without the intervention. In practice this would involve:

- baseline measure of ability (e.g. RA) for each participant;
- using the test manual to predict what their level would be after the intervention period (e.g. looking up the RA for a child at the 2nd centile in six months' time);
- running the intervention programme;
- remeasuring to find post-intervention measures;
- improvement in progress would be the difference between the two scores (actual gain-predicted gain).

Comparative data between different studies or different interventions could be produced that takes into account the level of severity of difficulty of the participants by calculating an Improvement Ratio Gain:

$$\text{Improvement ratio gain} = \frac{\begin{array}{c}\textbf{Actual gain} \\ \text{(Actual post-intervention} \\ \text{measure} - \text{baseline score)}\end{array} - \begin{array}{c}\textbf{Predicted gain} \\ \text{(Predicted post-intervention} \\ \text{measure} - \text{baseline score)}\end{array}}{\textbf{Time} \text{ spent on intervention programme}}$$

For some children, progress is so slow that trying to measure it using psychometric tests is difficult:

- Progress remains 'similar to that of peers starting from the same attainment baseline, but less than the majority of peers'. This definition effectively deals with the difficulties presented by the last definition. But it raises new questions. In the example of a poor reader our first question is how much progress should a similar child make in reading? This depends on the test and on the aspect of reading being considered. The table shows the amount of progress that 7-year-old children of different abilities should make when measured on the Neale Analysis of Reading Ability (NARA-II, Form 1) (Neale, 1997).

Reading skill	2nd centile child	4th centile child	16th centile child	50th centile child
Comprehension	Not measurable	Not measurable	9 months' progress	12 months' progress
Reading accuracy	Not measurable	Not measurable	7 months' progress	12 months' progress

What this table shows is that for a child who is low average, their progress will be less than one month for each month of teaching. The gap between them and the 50th centile child increases at a rate of five months per year for accuracy. For children at the bottom end of the spectrum, progress ceases to be measurable using a standardized test.

This difficulty of measuring adequate progress on standardized tests is recognized in part with the definition that uses:

- 'Matches or betters' previous progress. At the extreme end of the ability spectrum this could mean that the child learned two words last year and has mastered three this year.

Finally, the definition that tries to place teaching as a property of the child's learning in the given educational setting states:

- Ensures access to the full curriculum. The level of the curriculum is not specified and this means that access is determined by how well the teacher can teach and how well the curriculum is broken down. How much differentiation is needed? When does differentiation become modification?

The defining of adequate progress sets the inclusive context. Teachers are being presented with the task of including pupils as fully as possible within the curriculum. In order for it to be said that teaching has taken place, there must be evidence of learning. In order to demonstrate learning we need to take the following into account:

- All children are different and learn at different rates.
- There will always be fast learners and slow learners.
- Increasingly, the spectrum of children with difficulties in different areas will become more diverse as there is a move towards more inclusive learning.
- When we think about a child's progress we need to consider this and compare the child to similar children rather than 'average' children.
- When a child cannot learn as quickly as the majority of their peers then the teacher can increase remedial teaching; consider how to support children accessing the curriculum in their class at the planning stage of lesson preparation; or, do both of these.

IEPs and beyond SMART targets

Most schools have developed their own format for setting out individual education plans or they make use of a standard format produced by their LEA. The model in the Code of Practice uses the IEP to guide remedial teaching. An example format is shown on page 49.

There is a wide variety of practice when using IEPs. I have seen IEPs from some schools that include over 20 targets and have been set up in September to run through the school year. It is unlikely that the teacher can deal with so many targets, especially as there will be more than one pupil in the class needing an IEP.

Sometimes targets are woolly and are couched in terms that are unrealistic, e.g. *'the pupil's reading age will increase by six months in the next four weeks'*. Sometimes targets on the IEP reflect teaching targets for the curriculum being presented to the class. This is not necessary – IEPs should only include targets that are *different* and *additional*.

Good practice requires some prioritization. The IEP is usually devised for a short period of time and has three or four short-term targets that are:

- **S**pecific
- **M**easurable
- **A**ttainable
- **R**elevant
- **T**ime limited.

Ideally, the IEP should be set up with parents involved as equal partners. The pupil should also be able to give their views and have these included in the planning.

The strategies should involve highly structured programmes that are carried out frequently. They should have an emphasis on success, work to develop mastery learning and include some element of interleaved learning. Interleaved learning allows some previously learned material to be included when learning new material and has two advantages:

- It increases the child's confidence because the material is familiar and they succeed easily.
- It refreshes learning after a period when the skill or material has not been practised. This deals with the problem of children appearing to forget a skill that they had previously mastered. Relearning is usually quicker than the original learning and this suggests that something of the original memory may remain.

How the teaching is to be resourced is an important issue. There are several questions to be answered:

- **What** is to be used? What materials or learning packages are needed?
- **Who** is going to carry out the intervention?
- **When** is the remedial work going to be done?
- **How long** is going to be spent during each session on this strategy?
- **How often** is the strategy going to be used?

Monitoring of learning is important. It allows us to know whether the strategy chosen is effective or not. It also provides useful information about when a target has been reached and it is time to move on. The monitoring does not need to be carried out every time learning takes place but it should be built into the programme at regular intervals. Good monitoring allows the rate of progress to be gauged and this can help future planning.

Exit criteria simply state the level to which the skill has to be mastered before the target is considered to have been met. This means that either a new target can be set or the time for remedial teaching can be divided among the remaining targets to provide a more focused intervention.

In-class support

The second aspect of supporting children with dyslexia requires teachers to plan to go beyond the IEP. The two main features to include are:

- opportunities for generalization from remedial teaching to classroom work;
- classroom support strategies to be used.

The main difficulty is that the support strategies need to be communicated, in an efficient way, to all those people who will teach the child. In a secondary school, this may be 12 or 15 different teachers.

Arrangements also need to be in place for days when the usual teacher is absent or out on a training course.

Generalization is helped with good liaison between the teacher and adults working with the child on remedial programmes (either on a withdrawal basis, small-group basis or in teaching specific strategies in the classroom by working alongside the child).

The support strategies used in class can be drawn from the examples given in this book. They could also include a listing of useful aids, software and classroom support packages. As with the IEP, this sheet should only list those strategies that are not in common use in the classroom. As teachers become more familiar with the strategies that can be used to support dyslexic children in their classroom, the number of strategies needing to be recorded will be reduced.

The classroom support plan on page 50 gives a possible format for sharing this information and serves as an aide-mémoire for planning lessons. Ideally, it would be photocopied on to the back of the IEP. Most importantly, it is a working document to support the child in the classroom and as such should be referred to by the teacher during every lesson.

The classroom support plan will probably be longer term than the IEP. However, as with the IEP, it will need to be reviewed. Some strategies selected for the pupil may turn out to be ineffective; others may become redundant as the child makes progress.

Individual Education Plan

Pupil name

Concern that has been prioritized

Start date

End date

Target	Strategies	Resources	Monitoring arrangements	Exit criteria

Classroom Support Plan		
Pupil name	Start date	End date
Opportunities for generalization		
Useful information that the class teacher or subject teacher can collect to support specialist teaching		
Technological aids		
Classroom strategies		

The following example shows how the IEP and classroom support plan might be used together. This is not intended to be a perfect example, it is given to model how the forms could be used.

Harry is an 8-year-old. His teacher thinks that he is 'quite bright' and cites him being able to answer questions in class discussions and having a good memory for facts. He can easily alliterate and rime and seems to have a good phonological awareness – so long as no print is involved. In his reading, he often confuses similar looking letters. A piece of recent writing gives an idea of his spelling – 'i ga naw on a dus' [I go home on a bus]. At first these spellings appear bizarre. However, a closer look shows that he:

- confuses similar looking letters by orientation (b/d, h/n, w/m);
- confuses similar shaped letters (a/o);
- has not learned the orthographic rule for adding 'e' to make a long vowel sound (magic e rule).

Harry does not have a Statement and is currently supported at School Action Plus. His parents are very supportive, but busy and can only afford a few minutes each day to work with him. His mum is quite anxious that Harry 'plays her up' when she tries to work with him on reading and spelling.

A number of possibilities exist for choosing targets for Harry:

- improving discrimination between similar-looking letters when reading;
- improving discrimination between similar-looking letters when writing;
- learning specific words to improve reading and spelling (e.g. bus, home);
- working on the 'magic e rule';
- learning rules to help with all long vowel sounds;
- learning more general orthographic rules;
- develop proof-reading skills involving looking up words in a personal dictionary or word list.

These would be discussed between his teacher and parents at a planning meeting and a choice made. Once targets have been selected, materials are considered and strategies chosen. Monitoring is considered and exit criteria determined. The work of teaching Harry is then divided up.

The difficulty that Harry has in recording his ideas independently in class work is recognized and his teacher considers ways that might support him in class. The combined plan is shown on the next two pages.

Individual Education Plan

Pupil name   *Harry*   Start date   *1 Sep 06*   End date   *18 Oct 06*

Concern that has been prioritized

Harry confuses similar looking letters when reading and spelling

Target	Strategies	Resources	Monitoring arrangements	Exit criteria
Be able to discriminate between b/d when writing	Daily practice of 10 words chosen from list for quick spelling test with parents at home (M, T, W), adult helper during registration (Th, F)	Spelling lists of phonically regular words containing b/d	Score from Friday spelling tests	10 out of 10 on two successive weeks
Be able to discriminate between b/d/p/q and between h/n when reading	Daily practice of letter recognition with teaching assistant after break each afternoon	Precision teaching charts with randomly presented target letters produced on computer and printed on sheets. Stopwatch for timing one minute for fluency training	Weekly probe sheets to measure number of letters correctly identified in one minute	30 letters identified correctly in one minute on two successive probe sheets
Successfully identify b/d in class reading book	Peer tutoring with instruction to look for 'b' and 'd', daily before lunch	More competent peer trained to engage in peer tutoring and instructed in searching for 'b' and 'd'	Weekly check by teaching assistant and recorded to show percentage of letters identified	85% accuracy in spotting b/d correctly

Classroom Support Plan
Pupil name   *Harry*   Start date *1 Sep 06*   End date *Dec 06*

Opportunities for generalization	Looking for b/d during literacy hour whole-class reading, group reading and supported individual reading Targeted marking of writing to highlight b/d errors Teacher modelling choosing b/d in whole-class teaching and teaching mnemonic using hands to make letters
Useful information that the class teacher or subject teacher can collect to support specialist teaching	Evidence from targeted marking to inform choice of b/d words for practice spellings at home
Technological aids	b/d visual mnemonic cue cards sellotaped to corner of desk Electronic spell checker to allow Harry to check some words for himself Tape recorder so that the teacher can record reading to support Harry during classwork Tape recorder so that Harry can record some of his answers and ideas rather than writing them down
Classroom strategies	Sit near front so that teacher can easily provide support during reading or writing. Provide support 'in passing' Sit next to more competent peer (John) to support class reading and following worksheet instructions Being allowed to stick worksheets into book and writing short answers to questions directly on to sheet Cloze procedure for some writing Introducing Harry to the idea of the 'magic line' to encourage independent writing Personalized word list to copy words from during independent writing Key words put on board during class discussion about writing Key words for different curriculum areas displayed on walls, along with routine words such as days of the week

Differentiation

Children learn at different rates and this needs to be reflected in the approach taken by teachers and teaching assistants. The slower readers and spellers need more support while the faster readers and spellers need extending and pushing. This is referred to as differentiation within the classroom and can take many forms:

- *Differentiation by task* – different groups of children within the classroom are given different tasks linked to the teaching theme for the lesson.
- *Differentiation by outcome* – all the children are given the same task but expected to vary in the quality, length or complexity of response. If the task is to record thoughts and discussions about a character in a book, for example, some pupils may write several paragraphs of prose, others may make a list or a mind-map, or sketch an illuminating scene from the book.
- *Differentiation by support* – all the children get the same task and are expected to complete it to a similar standard but some children get more support than others. This support could include adding structure to the task (e.g. using writing frames) or could be adult support to complete some parts of the task. Group working allows children to support each other, e.g. a dyslexic child might be supported by a more competent reader who might in turn benefit from the scintillating array of ideas generated by the dyslexic child. Technological support can be used to enable a poor reader to access text more successfully or a poor writer to record ideas more independently. The next chapter contains ideas that teachers and parents can use to support their children.

The amount of support provided needs to be sufficient for the child to succeed but not so much so that it prevents the child from becoming an independent learner.

Learned helplessness

Some pupils appear to over-rely on adult support, waiting until the teacher or assistant is working with them before attempting things well within their capability. They become dependent on being 'led by the nose' and this reduces their ability to learn and problem solve. This learned helplessness is often associated with faulty beliefs such as, *'I must not be able to do it otherwise Miss would not be helping me. After all, she doesn't help anyone else!'*

In order to prevent this from happening it is necessary for the person supporting the child (teacher, teaching assistant, parent helper or parent) to consider a range of questions. This will allow effective support without encouraging dependency.

- Can I support a small group of children rather than an individual?
- Can I ask questions that prompt the children to think about strategies to use in order to solve the problem for themselves?
- How can I direct their attention to the important features of words when reading?
- How can I encourage them to make comparisons with words that they already know?
- Can I encourage them to take risks with learning, e.g. by guessing, praise their attempts, and show them where they have been successful (even if only partially)?
- Am I emotionally strong enough to refuse to help a child when I know that the task is well within their capability? Good monitoring of children's performance will allow me to remind the child of other occasions when they were able to do this task.
- How can I fade support as the child becomes more competent so that I am only providing the minimum level of help and encouraging the child to be independent? Can I leave the child longer before providing input, while at the same time expressing an expectation that they will successfully complete at least part of the task unaided?
- Can I make use of flow charts to take the child through routine procedures to increase the amount of time spent working independently? (Pictograms and teaching how to use the chart will decrease reliance on reading instructions or on adult support.)
- Can I make use of forward chaining? This is where the child starts off the first few steps of the problem and the adult helps them complete it. Gradually increasing the number of steps that the child is asked to do moves them towards greater independence.
- Can I make use of backwards chaining? In this case, the adult starts off the problem-solving, leaving the child to complete the last few steps. As with forward chaining, gradually increasing the number of steps that the child is asked to do moves them towards greater independence.

Examples of chaining include encouraging children to try out spellings by getting them to write down as much of the word as they can remember and replace missing parts with dashes. In free writing, some teachers make use of a 'magic line'. This simply allows the child to write the words that they think they know and to use a *magic line* to represent the words that they do not know. This has the advantage of maintaining a flow in writing, supporting self-esteem and allowing the teacher to provide guided assistance after the initial draft.

Comparison with peers

Children do not like to be seen to be different from their peers. This is a problem that seems to become more acute as they reach adolescence. This has three major effects in school:

- The child compares himself to peers in terms of performance, particularly in literacy, and often finds himself wanting.
- The child does not want to be singled out in class by having a 'helper' sit with him.
- It can be difficult to make, and keep, friends.

In the first case, the child's self-esteem can be protected by having a positive class ethos in which each child is valued for what they can do. The teacher is able to show the child in a positive light in classroom activities and allow the child to demonstrate competence in some activities in front of their peers. The teacher tries hard to avoid depreciating remarks that carry the messages *'You are useless/worthless'*.

Parents and carers have a role to play in this as well. It is easy for parents' anxieties and worries about a lack of progress to be contained in unintentional messages to the child. This might be because the child sees the parent is always at school talking to the teacher and having 'worried conversations'. In some schools this is mitigated by having an open atmosphere where parents regularly meet with teachers at the end of the day. In this case the child could be given a task to do while the parent and teacher talk. Another strategy is to have a home-school book in which positive comments and concerns are exchanged. Not all parents find it easy to visit school to talk about their child, especially when 'unknown' specialists are involved (SENCo, specialist teacher, school nurse, educational psychologist, etc.). Care should be taken to arrange such meetings at a time convenient to the parent, for example just after dropping their child at school or just before picking them up at the end of the day. Creating an informal and comfortable meeting place will put parents at ease and help to reassure them that their contribution is valued.

At home, parents should avoid talking to friends and relatives about the child's 'problems' while the child is listening. It is a natural response to a concern to want to talk it over with someone, but allowing the child to hear that his parents are worried, and giving him the impression that the 'whole world' knows about his failings, will not be very constructive.

The Code of Practice for Special Educational Needs places an emphasis on children being involved in their assessment and having a voice in reviews. This could be managed by having the child present as an equal partner in review meetings and having a discussion with a positive framing. This means that positive messages are used that focus on success – what can the child do today that he could not do last week?

In some schools, teachers use a 'dartboard' approach where each child sets one or two targets at a time. They write these on slips of paper with their name and pin them round the edge of the dartboard. They might be things such as:

- I want to read out loud in assembly by the end of term.
- I want to go up a level in mathematics by Christmas.
- I want to manage two weeks without detention.

As the children make progress, they move the targets closer to the bull's eye. Once they succeed, they write another target. This approach needs some negotiation with teachers and teaching assistants so that targets are realistic and achievable but it helps by encouraging the child to set goals and to monitor them. It also allows all the children in the class to set their own personal targets and this is supportive because it is the 'normal thing' to do. A second advantage of this approach is that it can also alert the teacher to what is important to the child. In the first example given above, it had never occurred to the teacher that the child might want to read in assembly as he had always appeared to be disaffected and sardonic.

Summary

In designing a remedial programme and planning classroom support think about:

- Where is the child starting from? What can he do already?
- What are his strengths and weaknesses?
- Are there opportunities for over-learning and interleaved learning?
- How will learning be linked between the remedial programme and everyday classroom work in order to support generalization?
- How does the remedial programme link to what the child needs in the classroom?
- How are links made between support staff and class or subject teachers?
- How can learning be 'fun'? For example, is there a variety of activities to teach the same knowledge or skills in a range of different ways?
- Who will do what and when will they do it?
- What specialist materials are needed?

3 | Classroom Settings and Supportive Strategies

The classroom environment

> John is writing a story. He wants to use a word that he is not sure about. He starts to look around the classroom where his teacher has placed 'key words' on almost every available surface. They appear on cupboards identifying their contents. They are hung on the wall naming the days of the week, months and seasons. They are displayed on the topic board – giving the specialist vocabulary needed for this term.

John's experience is a good example of how a teacher can create a supportive classroom environment. In a primary school, clear labelling of objects with pictograms as well as word labels will help with:

- acquiring reading skills of basic words used regularly in class;
- providing a model to support writing of familiar everyday words;
- allowing pupils to find things easily and independently.

In a secondary school, the classroom is more likely to be used for only one or two subjects and this means that subject-specific key words can be used. For instance in a science laboratory diagrams of each piece of commonly used equipment can be labelled as a model for pupils to use when writing up lab reports.

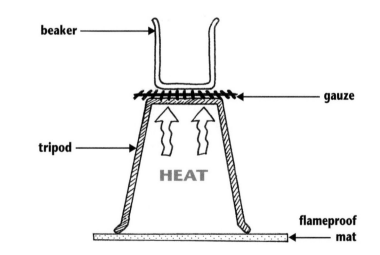

Other things to think about are:

- access to different resources within the classroom
  - word banks
  - spelling aids
  - a computer

- books of different reading ages covering the same content range
  - different types of pens/pencils
- location of aids to support dictionary skills and counting
  - alphabet arcs or lines
  - number lines
  - multiplication squares
- aids to remembering common sequences
  - days of the week
  - months of the year.

Children will still need to be encouraged to make use of the information around them and further support might be needed.

Adult support

A range of adults can provide support in the classroom but the responsibility for teaching or co-ordinating teaching lies with the class teacher.

Classes vary in size and the amount of adult support available varies. Some classes may have fewer than 20 pupils while others will be over 30. Some classes will have only one teacher while others will have teaching assistants, parent helpers and other volunteers.

Fortunately, very few children require one-to-one support all of the time. This means that a range of strategies can be used:

- The teacher can circulate around the class rather than remaining at a fixed workstation. This allows for frequent but short visits to ensure that the child is still coping with the reading or writing task. Short prompts can be given in passing and the child reassured frequently.
- Direct support through assisted writing or acting as a scribe or a reader.
- Reading through written feedback with the child so that they are aware of the comments made by the teacher.
- Giving help with spelling words that they are unsure about.
- Repeating significant points of the lesson in different forms, e.g. providing structured verbal questions or additional discussion that allows the child to explore concepts at a different level.
- One-to-one discussion can provide different angles to get the same point across.
- Adult support might be needed for assessment in key subjects.
- Support can be used to provide regular reinforcement of new skills/knowledge or skills taught in remedial work to encourage generalization.

Peer support

A shortage of adult time does not mean that children cannot be supported in class. A more competent peer can sometimes be used to support a weaker child. This could include:

- paired reading
- acting as a reader
- acting as a scribe
- acting as a checker, e.g. proof-reading the child's script and identifying three spelling errors, or as a 'critical friend'
- as a 'tester' for spellings, etc.

With a positive and supportive ethos operating in the classroom, the more competent child can act as a role model for the dyslexic child in order to support literacy development. Care needs to be taken in the choice of 'pairings' for this purpose however, and some sort of preparation or training for the 'peer tutor' is advisable. Consideration should be given by the 'peer tutor' to having a positive approach at all times, and knowing how to help without 'doing it for him'.

Often, the dyslexic child will be able to do some things better than the child supporting him with reading, and this means that the support is able to flow in both directions. Care should be taken that the arrangement does not in any way disadvantage the more able pupil, as outlined in this parent's views:

'Richard was always good at science, top of the class. But he was paired up with a dyslexic boy and always had to help him. I felt that he should have been doing extension work, more challenging stuff to keep him interested and stretch him. But he was always saddled with John, and often ended up spending his breaktimes helping him to finish off his work.'

Seating

Should the teacher sit all children with special needs on one table so that she can spend more time with them as a group? At face value this seems to have clear advantages, however, it can mean that dyslexic children are not suitably challenged – they need support with literacy while being given content that is demanding. The danger of having all children with SEN on one table is that opportunities for presenting more demanding work are lost.

The alternative is to sit children in mixed-ability groupings. This has the advantage of providing more appropriate social mixes and allowing the dyslexic child to access complex work with peers. If the child is sitting with other children of the same intellectual ability then they can participate in discussions at an appropriate level. This may also be protective of self-esteem for a bright dyslexic child.

The disadvantage is that the teacher has to move about more in order to provide support for reading and writing.

The following strategies might help:

- Sit the child near to the teacher's table to allow easy access to adult support and to allow the teacher to monitor progress.
- Sit the child near to, and facing the board to help with:
  - copying, by reducing the time taken from looking at the target information and writing it down (helps reduce working memory demands);
  - providing good literacy models from the class teacher;
  - providing a clear focus for board-based explanations.
- Position the child near to/in clear sight of displayed flow diagrams and key words to support instruction-following and extended writing.

If the child is left-handed, consideration will need to be given about whom the child sits next to and on which side. It is easy for left- and right-handed children to be placed next to each other so that they tend to crowd each other out when writing. (Left-handers need to have extra 'elbow room' on their left side, so should always sit to the left of a right-handed classmate.) The teacher will need to ensure that there is sufficient room for children to sit with correct posture and balance when writing and have sufficient space to place reference materials.

Coloured overlays

Coloured overlays can help some dyslexic children and it is always worth keeping some in the classroom. These are clear sheets of plastic, like OHP transparencies, in a range of colours. They work by changing the background colour of the text and reducing the high contrast between print and paper. When these are placed over the text, some pupils say, *'The words have stopped jumping about!'* Research indicates that many students read more quickly and effectively using the overlays.

Access to text on the computer

If black print on a white background is proving a problem, change the colours on the word processor. Right click on an empty area on the desktop. This will bring up a menu; click on *Properties* to open up the *Display Properties* window. Click on the *Appearance* tab and in the *Item* box, choose *Window*. You can now choose different colours for text and background. Black text on a grey background is less painful to the eyes than the standard white 'paper' but each user may have different preferences. It is quick and easy to change colours.

Research
Arnold Wilkins has undertaken a controlled experiment using a Colorimeter to investigate the effects of coloured lenses and overlays on dyslexia. The Colorimeter allows a child to select the colour that they find most useful in reducing any effects of glare. This can be used as a coloured overlay or built into a pair of coloured glasses. Wilkins showed that coloured overlays increase the rate of reading and reduce visual stress, even in children with no known deficit within the school system.
Using a Rate of Reading test, in which 15 common words are presented in random order, children who chose to use a coloured overlay read faster. More than 50% of the children reported improved perception with coloured filters, and 47% chose the same colour in response to different assessment methods and examiners. Their improvement in reading fluency persisted at retest.
http://www.essex.ac. uk/psychology/overlays/

Visit Ian Jordan's website: www. visualdyslexia.com

A company called Tintavision has been trialling 'asfedic tuning' with a small number of schools. This is a process designed to rapidly improve a person's reading speed, accuracy and stamina by finding the most appropriate filter. Specialist software is used to find the exact shade of filter from some 16 million choices, to maximize the rate of reading and reading stamina. The company provides a filter and arranges return visits where the filters will be changed after further testing. In time, many pupils have reached a stage where they can read efficiently without filters of any kind as their eyes are tuned to deal with the text they meet in day-to-day life.
Tel: 01778 349 233;
Fax: 01778 345 599;
www.tintavision.com

What else can be provided?

There is a range of devices that might help. One example is the Visual Tracking Magnifier (VTM), designed by Ian Jordan and produced by Combined Optical industries, which won a Millennium Award. It is a magnifying glass with a clear window across the centre for viewing groups of words and a patterned area above and below to block out interference from surrounding text.

The VTM is easily tracked across a page and works by eliminating the pattern glare that confuses visual dyslexics. It also increases spatial differences between lines.

It consists of a specially designed pattern printed onto a bright field magnifying glass. A central clear rotatable band magnifies words so that they can be easily broken into their component parts.

The device should assist nearly all early readers struggling with the mechanics of reading and a proportion of older pupils with difficulties.

The VTM is designed to reduce pattern glare without the use of tints. It aids fixation and may promote 'good' saccadal eye movement. Flicker is also reduced ... It could be used in conjunction with other treatments, tinted spectacles for example.
Jordan, 2000

Where pupils are benefiting from using overlays, it might be worth considering the Optim-Eyes™ Task Lamp, also produced by Ian Jordan. Overlays are useful for reading but may not help the pupil who needs to compose and review what he has written.

The Optim-Eyes™ lamp is colour selectable, allowing colours to be mixed to create the optimum lighting to suit each user. The lamp can be used in addition to specifically prescribed tinted spectacles to achieve optimum results. The colour selection can be operated either individually or together so that it is possible to select single primary colours or combine them to give different hues and luminance that can be used for both reading and writing.
Jordan, 2000

Supportive strategies

How can pupils with reading and spelling difficulties be supported in mainstream classrooms and included in the curriculum? Ofsted (1999) surveyed over 50 schools and found that pupils' responses were better when teachers understood the difficulties of the children and made allowances for this in the work presented and in their teaching style. Where the quality of teaching was unsatisfactory it was because the teachers had unrealistic expectations of what the children could read and how much of their understanding they could demonstrate in writing. When teachers received training and support they were better able to take difficulties into account and plan appropriately for the pupils. This echoes a theme from the Code of Practice for SEN – teachers notice children's difficulties and respond by adjusting their teaching appropriately.

There are many things that teachers can do for pupils in every lesson to support literacy. Cooper and McIntyre (1993) found a number of commonalities between pupil perceptions and teacher perceptions of effective classroom practice. Ofsted (1999) found similar effective practices being used with children who did not have direct support through a Statement of SEN. Some of these are relevant to supporting pupils with reading and writing difficulties:

- teacher discussions (recapping from previous lessons; story-telling; leading class discussions; teacher explanations; teacher exposition of ideas);
- use of the board (notes and diagrams as an aide-mémoire);
- use of pictures and other visual stimuli (including video material).

In this chapter we are going to present a range of ways of responding to children's needs. Not all the strategies will be needed with all children, but there are sufficient ideas to allow a graduated response.

Supporting classroom reading

Teachers can support children with literacy difficulties by carefully selecting books for them and by thinking about how text is used when preparing worksheets. Text can be differentiated in a number of ways:

Language structure

Think about the language structure used in the books, worksheets, computer programs and board work used with the child. Is it at a level that they can cope with? Many of the indices for measuring reading ages of text consider sentence length, syllable counts and word familiarity. This is because:

- Long sentences are harder to read than short ones. More demand is made on the memory to hold on to the ideas contained in the sentence. This means that less use can be made of sentence context to predict what the next words will be.
- High-frequency words are encountered more often in reading and are more likely to be in the child's vocabulary.
- Longer words place more demands on auditory memory for beginner readers than short words. Polysyllabic words make more

demands on working memory for children who have learned to chunk letters into sound groups.

- Active verbs are easier to understand than passive verbs. Whether a verb is active or passive depends on how it is used in the sentence. For example, both the following sentences mean the same but the first one is easier to read and understand:
  - The cat chased the dog. (Active)
  - The dog was chased by the cat. (Passive)

Emotional impact

Tightly packed text can be overwhelming to a child who is struggling with reading. They see a lot of words on the page and somehow they have to make sense of what is being said. This can be so off-putting that the child tries to avoid the task. The equivalent experience for an adult would be a bit like reading a very academic, theoretical book on dyslexia! The following suggestions will help to make it easier (and some have been employed in thinking about this book):

- *Small blocks of text with spaces clearly defined.* This includes the use of:
  - Paragraphs – white space is important. As well as separating ideas, it gives emotional reassurance – the page becomes a set of little chunks to be read.
  - Boxes and frames – separate out ideas or functions within the text. For example, have instructions in one box and an explanation in another.
  - Colour-coding of text – can make it easier for the teacher or parent to guide the child, *'just read the blue bit'*.
  - Use of bullet points and lists rather than continuous prose – helps present ideas quickly without wasting time decoding text that carries no information other than the niceties of the English language.
  - Use of diagrams and pictures – breaks up the text. These also convey important visual information that can help children to quickly understand the relationships between ideas and how these relate to the text. Pictures need to be chosen carefully so that they do not distract. They can be humorous, and may be the first thing that the child looks at – they act to draw the child into the book or worksheet.
- *Larger text.* This can give the child the feeling of moving swiftly through a page or book.
- *The look of the book.* Many dyslexic children are aware of their difficulties with reading and believe that other children will think they are stupid if they cannot read the same books as the rest of the class. This is made worse if they are reading books intended for younger pupils, especially if they are in a junior class reading an infant book. Teachers can make use of 'parallel readers' – books not used in school for the majority of readers but saved for those who need extra practice at every stage.

Checking text readability

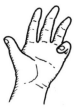

The Five Finger test

This is a quick way to check the suitability of a book for a child. It is not foolproof, but is easy enough for children to learn themselves and employ when choosing a book from the library, class reading box or bookshop. It works with 'chapter books' where there are more than just a couple of sentences on a page. Choose a page in the middle of the book, ask the child to read the text out loud. Each time he comes across a word that he cannot read, tell him the word and count the word with a finger. If you run out of fingers before you reach the end of the page then the text is probably too hard.

Use a word processor to check reading ages

You could scan or type the text into a word processor and then use the in-built readability statistics to tell you the reading age. In Word, go to the Tools menu, click Options, then click the Spelling and Grammar tab. Select the Check grammar with spelling check box. Select Show the readability statistics check box, then click OK. Click Spelling and Grammar on the Standard toolbar. When Word finishes checking spelling and grammar, it displays information about readability of the text.

The **Flesch-Kincaid Grade Level** is reported by Microsoft Word. The number given is the average reading ability for pupils in the school year in the US education system. Adding 5 to the number produces a reading age. It can be calculated by hand using the following steps:

1. Count the number of words in the sample.
2. Count how many sentences are in the sample.
3. Find the average sentence length by dividing the number of words by the number of sentences.
4. Now multiply this number by 0.39.
5. Count the number of syllables in the sample.
6. Divide the number of syllables by the number of words.
7. Multiply this number by 11.8.
8. Add your answer from step 4 to your answer from step 7, then subtract 15.59 to get the grade level.
9. Add 5 to get the reading age.

There are many ways of calculating reading ages. A slightly simpler way than the previous example is the **Fog Index**. This tends to work better with older pupils:

1. Open the book randomly at three different places and count 100 words in each place to give three samples.
2. Count how many sentences there are in each sample. For incomplete sentences, estimate how much of the remaining sentence in each sample is included in the sample (to the nearest tenth).
3. Work out the average sentence length by dividing 300 by the total number of sentences in the three samples.
4. Count how many words have three or more syllables in the three samples. Divide this number by 3 (to give an average).
5. Add together your answers from step 3 and step 4.
6. Multiply this by 0.4 to get the grade level.
7. Add 5 to get the reading age.

Sources of suitable readers

A much easier way is to look at publishers' websites to see suggested age ranges of different books. Look out for 'High interest, low reading ages'. These are designed to motivate older readers while still having a low reading age.

The Dyslexia Institute also lists hundreds of books suitable for dyslexic readers. Tel: 01784 463 851 or email: info@dyslexia-inst.org.uk

A graded list of reading books is available from the National Association for Special Educational Needs. Tel: 01827 311 500 or email: welcome@nasen.org.uk

Aaron is a Year 5 pupil whom I observed in class. The pupils were spending ten minutes quietly reading while the teacher took the register and got materials ready for a science lesson.

Aaron had taken out a thick tome – Harry Potter. Other children on the table were reading similar books and he desperately wanted to read it. The book was far too difficult for Aaron and he spent most of the time looking around the classroom, flicking backwards and forwards through the pages and fiddling with his pencils.

His teacher noticed and asked him to take out his 'reading book'. Instead of a thick paperback book like the other children had, out came a thin hardback from the school's reading scheme. The book is just at a level that Aaron can read – but he doesn't want to. It is not what the other children are reading about. How many 9-year-olds want to read a story written for 6-year-olds? Aaron laid it on his table and volunteered to help give out equipment.

Competency and reading

The demands of the text need to be matched to the abilities of the child. The teacher reflects on whether or not the child can read 90% of a sample of the text without direct support. At this level, the child will encounter 2 words out of every 20 that are 'difficult'. He will be able to decode sufficient information to make use of sentence meaning and word attack skills to make a reasonable guess at the word. This is how competent readers become better readers.

Exposure to print for a child who has grasped the basics means that he can learn more about reading and increase his sight vocabulary, reading fluency and verbal repertoire through reading. The difficulty for the teacher of a dyslexic child is providing text at a reading level that allows this level of accuracy, while also being meaningful to the lesson or to the child. There are a number of reading schemes available that have high interest levels but low reading ages for older children with reading difficulties.

Improving worksheet layout to support reading

All the principles that apply to selecting books for children also apply to worksheet design. When designing a worksheet, the teacher can think about:

- Breaking up large chunks of text. Have plenty of sub-headings as signposts and markers. You can support organizational difficulties if questions related to the text are included in the same box, along with a space to write the answer. In comprehension exercises, this will also help children with working memory deficits by reducing the attentional capacity demands needed to remember the location of the text they were reading as they ponder the answer to the question asked. This will reduce the need to re-read the text from the beginning if the child suddenly loses their place. For example, instead of having three paragraphs of text and then six questions, split the text into paragraphs, with two questions placed under each. Each block can then be placed in a box to emphasize the structure of the information. Reading is supported because the child does not need to re-read the whole of the text in order to find the answers.

Text Text Text Text Text Text Text Text Text Text Text Text Text Text Text Text Text Text Text Text Text Text Text Text Text Text Text Text Text Text Text Text Text Text Text Text Text Text Text Text Text Text Text Text Text Text Text Text Text Question 1 Question 2 Question 3 Question 4 Question 5 Question 6	Text Text Text Text Text Text Text Text Text Text Text Text Text Text Question 1 Question 2
	Text Text Text Text Text Text Text Text Text Text Text Text Question 3 Question 4
	Text Text Text Text Text Text Text Text Text Text Text Text Text Text Text Text Question 5 Question 6

- Supporting text with visual cues, e.g. pictures, diagrams, flow charts.
- Making sure that sheets are typed rather than handwritten. This is to provide a consistent model of print for the child to recognize. Choose a font that is clear and easy to read. The most dyslexia-friendly are generally thought to be Arial, *Sassoon* and *Comic Sans*.
- Selecting a point size that is appropriate to the child. Use 12 or 14 point so that the pupil does not have to strain to read the words. Small text requires both eyes to scan and focus on a small area. Younger children find this difficult, as they have not yet developed ocular stability. In some older children, a lack of ocular stability makes the letters on the page appear to move. Enlarging the text provides a bigger target for both eyes to focus on.
- Avoiding justified margins.

Some pupils have major problems with 'channelling' – they are more aware of the spaces between the words than the words themselves. Textbooks and handouts frequently have justified margins to make the page look neat. These work by using irregular spacing between words, so there is a tidy right-hand margin. Where pupils have significant problems with tracking, or maintaining a smooth flow across a line of text, they are likely to find such pages harder to read.

Note the irregular spacing between words.

Some pupils have major problems with 'channelling' – they are more aware of the spaces between the words than the words themselves. Textbooks and handouts frequently have justified margins to make the page look neat. These work by using irregular spacing between words, so there is a tidy right-hand margin. Where pupils have significant problems with tracking, or maintaining a smooth flow across a line of text, they are likely to find such pages harder to read.

Worksheets that give instructions

If the worksheet is giving instructions for practical work, try to put each new instruction on a new line. Number the instructions to support the child's organization and memory. If possible support with pictures. See example on page 70.

Teacher strategies when working with the whole class

- Start by directing pupils' attention to the text to be read by holding the book up to the class and identifying the area to be read:
  - point at the target text;
  - identify the colour of text box;
  - state the paragraph number;
  - use other cues, e.g. "under the picture", "on the left page, half-way down", "just before the questions".
- Pre-read the text with the class so that the child feels more confident when approaching independent reading. This also allows the child to make use of memory strategies to reduce the need to rely on fluent reading.
- Carry out whole class discussion of the text prior to individual work.
- Use different coloured chalk or whiteboard markers with each line of writing to be copied from the board, to help the child scan and relocate the next target word to be written. If the child has

Growing plants

This week

You will need: a ruler, 2 plants about the same size, 2 labels.

1. Write 'Dark' on one label.
2. Measure one of the plants with a ruler.
3. Write the height of the plant in the table.
4. Put the label on to the pot.
5. Put the plant in a dark cupboard.
6. Write 'Light' on the other label.
7. Measure the other plant with a ruler.
8. Write the height into the table.
9. Put the label on to the pot.
10. Put the plant on the windowsill.
11. Leave for one week (make sure they both have enough water).

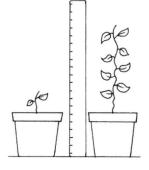

	Plant in **DARK** place	Plant in **LIGHT** place
Height at start		
Height after one week		

Next week

1. Measure each plant again.
2. Put the new heights into the table.

How much has each one grown?

difficulty remembering where they were up to, they may find it easier to remember that they were on the green line. Take care to check for contrast in different parts of the room and at different times of day – blue chalk on a blackboard looks fine until the sun shines on it! Alternatively, number each line of text.

Other strategies

- An adult can pre-read text with the pupil prior to use in the lesson so that the difficult bits are identified and dealt with. This then improves confidence for independent reading during the actual lesson. Parents can be involved in this type of support if there is good liaison between home and school. Parents could read with their child using a paired reading approach or an apprenticeship model approach (see page 135).
- The child can have direct support in class through assisted reading by the teacher, teaching assistant or a more competent peer.
- A computerized script reader can be used in class. This consists of special software to read text files from the computer. Some versions of this are available free from the Internet. The latest version of Microsoft Word includes a speech option that will enable the computer to read highlighted text. This could be used to read back the child's work or work prepared by the teacher. When linked with a scanner and used with Optical Character Recognition (OCR) software, it is possible to scan any text and have the computer read it out to the child. Although this software is good and getting better, it does have a number of disadvantages:
  - It needs a relatively fast machine to work on and older machines may not cope with the demands, or may read too slowly.
  - The voice is mechanical and often has an American accent.
  - Syllables are not emphasized naturally.
  - Initials, acronyms and compound words are incorrectly pronounced.

  These problems are not insurmountable, but require some time in training the child to use the software. The use of headphones is recommended to reduce distractions to the rest of the class, and to minimize interference from background noise.
- A ruler can be used to help with tracking in reading. A clear plastic ruler can be placed under the target text and this allows the child to see the next words on the line. It also allows the child to gauge how much of the page is left to read. A *linetracker* (LDA) does a similar job – possibly with more 'street cred'.
- A cardboard mask can be made that exposes one or two words at a time. This is useful if the child continues to have difficulty looking at the target word(s). A more sophisticated aid is the Jordan Visual Tracking Magnifier – a small lens that is placed over the target word to enlarge it and develop eye-tracking skills (see page 63).

Obtaining text to speech software

The following websites have versions of software available for converting text to speech:

www.ReadPlease.com
ReadPlease is a free download that works fine with highlighted text

www.elantts.com
Provides a demo version

www.infovox.se/demo. htm
Provides a demo version

www.loriens.com
A company that writes software specifically for dyslexics and has a demo version to try

- A photocopier can be used to enlarge text, which aids binocular control. A bigger target on the page helps children who say that they experience the words moving on the page. An A4 magnifier could be used instead – but check quality carefully as the prismatic effect can cause interference patterns that spoil the image and make reading more difficult.
- Some children can be helped when writing is on coloured paper. It might be worth experimenting to see if a particular shade or colour helps improve reading.
- Coloured overlays can also be used to help reduce apparent movement of letters. The *Irlen Test* is a test for scotopic sensitivity that can help identify which colour filter is best. Some ophthalmologists will do this test and will prescribe coloured lenses. The *Wilkins Rate of Reading Test* can be used to explore the type of overlay that works best for children in Years 4 to 6 (see page 62).
- A taped commentary of the class text being read can be provided so that the child can rewind and relisten to the text, e.g. during comprehension exercises.
- The child can record his own voice to help with reading and to use with word cards to support reading development (e.g. with the Language Master system).

The Language Master system is available from Drake Educational.
Tel: 029 2056 0333
www.drakegroup.co.uk

Strategies to help the child understand the purpose of reading and writing come from a simple mnemonic – the PQRS strategy for reading (Preview, Question, Read, Summarize):

- **Preview** – look over the text to see if there are clues as to what it is about. Picture clues, headings, boxes, etc. give a quick idea. With more competent readers this is developed into scanning and skimming skills.
- **Raise questions** to be answered. What do we want to find out? This might be very pertinent in looking for specific information from a textbook. With a story we might want to know what happens to the main character.
- **Read** the text. Expectations will already have been set up regarding what the text is about and this will help with predictive processing of which words might be coming next.
- **Summarize** – briefly say what the text was about. What are the answers to the questions that were raised? If it is a story, then use this time to set up expectations for the next reading session – what might happen next?

There are also specific skills needed to deal with challenging text:

- **Word-segmentation** – how can I break this word down? Are there any smaller words in it that I recognize? Are there groups of letters that I have seen before, e.g. 'ing', 'ed'?
- **Syntactic checking** – does the structure of the sentence, as I have read it, make sense?

- **Semantic checking** – does the meaning of the sentence, as I have read it, make sense?

Supporting classroom writing

How well should children be able to record information in writing and access ideas from text? There is an expectation that all children should reach a certain standard of achievement to be considered 'average'. Over the period 1948 to 1996, surveys of literacy standards in the UK carried out by the Assessment of Performance Unit show that very little change has occurred in literacy standards (Shiel, 2002). Data from SATs collected show a steady improvement during the introduction phase of the National Literacy Strategy followed by a plateau. The table shows the percentage of pupils achieving the expected standard of Level 4 at the end of Key Stage 2 (Ofsted, 2002, 2003). There continues to be a gap between boys and girls and writing continues to lag behind reading for both genders.

Pupils achieving Level 4 (or above)

Year	Reading		Writing	
	Girls	Boys	Girls	Boys
1999	82	75	62	47
2000	86	80	63	48
2001	85	78	65	50
2002	83	77	68	52
2003	84	78	69	52
2004	87	79	71	56

Percentage of children achieving the expected standard in reading at the end of Key Stage 2

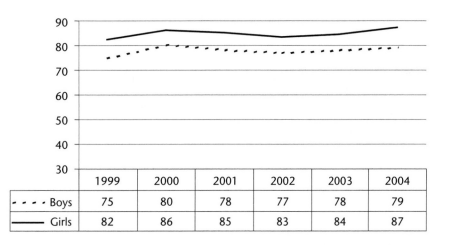

	1999	2000	2001	2002	2003	2004
- - - Boys	75	80	78	77	78	79
—— Girls	82	86	85	83	84	87

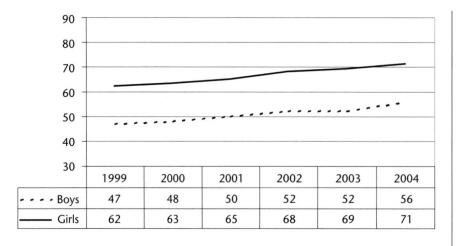

	1999	2000	2001	2002	2003	2004
- - - - Boys	47	48	50	52	52	56
—— Girls	62	63	65	68	69	71

Many children will not be able to write as well as expected of 'average' pupils, and will need supporting in class: this is particularly relevant to dyslexic pupils. Writing is a very complex process for anyone – even practised adults. This applies particularly to the production of a piece of creative or persuasive text. Preparation for this is all-important – the opportunity to think and talk about ideas, plan a sequence and research any unfamiliar spellings. The task of putting pen to paper is much more achievable when the child knows what he wants to 'say'. This sort of preparation can be done in a group but will be most effective when led by a teacher or teaching assistant.

- Ask the pupils to answer only half the questions on a comprehension exercise – all the odd numbers/all the even numbers/the first three and last three. Remember that the questions are likely to be gradated in difficulty so choose alternate questions in order to give the child a chance to think about the harder concepts as well as the easy ones.
- Have models of language on the walls and cupboards of the classroom.
- Provide common spelling lists of words used in each topic or have these specially prepared on word cards around the room.
- For some pupils this can be adapted to personal word banks. These can be in a format appropriate to the age and ability of the child – a little book, a tin, or envelope with words that they need to use or ask about frequently.
- In some classes, teachers have found it useful to have laminated sheets of high-frequency words in alphabetical order, which pupils can keep on their tables.
- Cue cards can help remind pupils of common mistakes that they make when writing.

Recording ideas and information in prose can move through a gradation:

- Voice recording, e.g. to a tape recorder.
- Dictation, e.g. to a peer or adult; to a computer with speech recognition software.
- Using copy-writing models, graduated from over-writing to under-writing.
- Copying.
- Using sentence makers – common words that the child needs are written on cards and the child assembles the sentence using the cards. The teacher checks the sentence and then the child copies the model into his book.
- Using disrupted information – instead of giving the child a block of text to copy, provide them with the sentences in a jumbled order. If the sentences are cut out before the lesson, they can reassemble the order, checking the sequence with an adult or peer, and then copy them. This allows the child to apply some thought to their writing while being supported.
- Copying the bulk of the text but completing missed-out bits, e.g. cloze procedure, sentence completion. This can be graduated further, e.g. providing the answers for the child to choose from; having source text containing the answers; having only a blank space to fill.
- Writing independently, using key words provided by the teacher. Support independent writing by providing key words on the board, on cupboards in the classroom, on topic boards, in subject-specific dictionaries.
- Writing to dictation.
- Writing independently with help to organize ideas, e.g. using writing frames, writing independently after planning.
- Totally independent writing.

Which　　　**Witch**

- If worksheets are used, then allow the child to write on the sheet, rather than copying into his book. This will help him to keep up with other children in the class by saving time re-reading and retracking the target text, and will help with slower writing speed and slower information processing speed.
- Reduce writing demands by teaching the child how to record information independently and effectively using mind-maps and flow diagrams.
- Use sentence completion by providing most of the sentence as a model with space for the child to complete it. Gradation could include providing the answers in a jumble, which the child selects.
- Give the child a book to make into a personalized dictionary. They write in the words that they want to use but frequently get wrong, or do not know. Teach them how to use the dictionary.
- Provide an alphabet line or alphabet arc to assist with independent dictionary skills:

Aa Bb Cc Dd Ee Ff Gg Hh Ii Jj Kk Ll Mm Nn Oo Pp Qq Rr Ss Tt Uu Vv Ww Xx Yy Zz

- Some children become over-reliant on phonic strategies and spell words as they sound. Try providing them with the *Aurally Coded English* (ACE) *Dictionary*. This allows the child to look up words as they sound and then to find the correct spelling.
- With more competent children, encourage proof-reading skills. Teach the children to check for spelling mistakes, grammar and then meaning. This is always easier to do with someone else's work than with your own. When you have written something, you know what it 'should' say! Train pupils to work with 'critical friends', where each checks the other's work.
- Encourage the use of an electronic spell-checker. These vary in complexity and price. The cheaper ones allow the child to type in the word as they think it should be typed and it then offers them several possibilities from which to choose. More expensive versions will provide definitions of the chosen word so that the child can check that they have the right meaning.
- Teach spelling as an integral part of every lesson.

There are several ways to record ideas and observations that involve very little writing, or none at all. The following were suggested by Year 6 children attending a centre for dyslexic pupils:

- Use a tape recorder.
- Take photos with a digital camera and add text.
- Use a video camera.
- Make a recording using a computer and web cam.
- Tell the teacher the answers.
- Make a storyboard.
- Make a poster.
- Record information in a table.

The use of technological aids is covered in Chapter 4.

Summary
There are many things that the teacher can do to make the classroom more 'dyslexia friendly'. This involves thinking about:

- the classroom environment
- how human resource support is organized
- how tasks can be supported and adjusted
- how information is organized

4 | Using ICT to Help Dyslexic Learners

Modern technology has much to offer to all children but is particularly valuable for dyslexic learners. Used wisely, it is highly motivating, time saving and enables pupils to produce work that looks extremely good. New hardware and software is being developed all the time, so it is worth exploring the market to keep abreast of new developments. A company such as Iansyst (http://www.dyslexic.com/) is a good place to start as their catalogue contains products from all the major providers and has plenty of examples of general and specialist technology. If possible, visit educational exhibitions during the year as this is a good opportunity to see products demonstrated or ask for advice about specific pupils' needs (BETT, January, London; Education Show, March, Birmingham NEC; Special Needs North, May, Bolton; Special Needs London, November, London).

Such technology can help build skills at word, sentence and text level. Teachers and parents often choose spelling programs as they are easy to use and can be fitted around other activities, but effective learning with ICT may have to start with the assessment of how the individual child learns best. For example, poor short-term memory can affect learning performance. In addition, it may be the cause of poor behaviour or attention-deficit problems. When learners cannot remember the task/word/instructions properly, they may develop avoidance strategies and act as the class clown.

Mastering Memory is a program from the Communication and Learning Skills Centre (CALSC, www.masteringmemory.co.uk or www.calsc. co.uk) that can be used to identify and extend particular strengths and learning styles. It can teach pupils strategies to improve auditory and visual memory and to build on their strengths as well. Research shows that after learning strategies such as rehearsing and repeating sequences, learners can improve both their long- and short-term memory which means that their time in the classroom will be more productive. Another useful program from CALSC is *Timely Reminders*, a framework that helps learners organize, review and revisit their work regularly. This is good practice for exams.

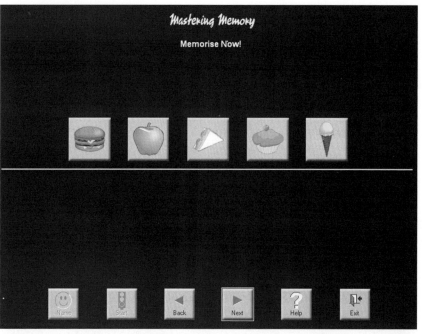

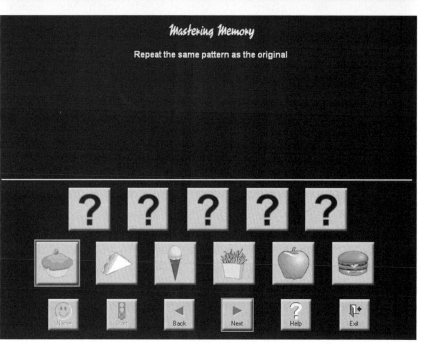

Figures used with permission from CALSC, PO Box 621, Sutton, Surrey SM1 2ZS

Brainstorming and structuring writing

Pupils with dyslexia are sometimes very good at talking and can expound at length. What they are not so good at is getting those thoughts on paper. Collaborative writing, writing frames, planning tools, postcards and Post-its can all be used to good effect. There is no reason why planning has to be in text form, however. Let the planning stage be in the form of drawings or symbols and move them around on the table so that the learner is working in a more holistic way and not always using linear structures. Pupils can easily add or delete text, always leaving a neat, clearly understandable diagram at the end. Use colour to link similar ideas.

There are also plenty of software programs for planning: *Inspiration* is a mind-mapping tool; *Draft Builder*, a planning tool with speech support and switch access; and *StarThink*, a new program from Fisher Marriott. Alternatively, one can use the outline facility in *Word* or an on-screen grid such as *Clicker* or *WordBar* that can be used for writing frames to scaffold work and create a structure. These contain structured phrases that characterize particular genres such as formulating an argument, describing a process or writing an email.

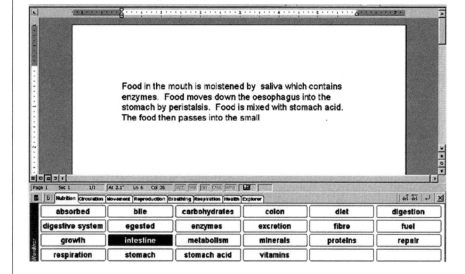

With a larger screen display or an interactive whiteboard, the whole class can work on a plan together that can be printed off for use in independent writing or for collaborative work with a small group. Interactive whiteboards can be an excellent classroom resource as they encourage pupils to contribute. Some teachers report that pupils are more active and alert in lessons where interactive whiteboards are used. This may be because they can engender a lot of movement with dragging, dropping and moving text and pictures or using animations.

The range of technology

- The use of **laptop computers** has revolutionized school life for some dyslexic learners. They are able to transport the machines from class to class and, with practice, become very proficient at using them.
- Use a **word processor** to allow the child to produce neat copies of work for display, to take home or to stick in a class book.
- You can use a **spell checker** to provide instant feedback on spelling errors and to allow the child to select from a restricted range of possibilities. If the child cannot get their ideas down because the spell checker distracts them and stops their flow of thoughts, then turn it off and teach the child the habit of spell checking once the document is written.

Some teachers like a structured programme that is based on rules or letter patterns using software such as *WordShark2, Eye for Spelling* or *I Can Spell* or *Magic –e* from Xavier. Many pupils see computers as patient and non-threatening. The software provides immediate feedback and many of the programs set out to make learning fun. Some spelling programs keep records but often the software works through a prescribed route so it is not necessarily an individualized programme of learning.

Word processing and spell checking in action

Matthew, aged 15, is working towards GCSE history. He has enjoyed the lessons as the teacher makes sure there is lots of discussion around the source documents. He is particularly good at finding clues in photographs and cartoons, which other pupils miss. He can also interpret graphs quite well. He has problems however, in producing written answers that do justice to his historical understanding and knowledge.

He is working on the question: 'Why did support for the Nazis increase in the period 1929–1933?'

The figure below shows Matthew's handwritten work. The deficiencies are obvious at a glance. It is untidy, the letters are not evenly formed, the spelling is weak and many common words such as 'people' are misspelt. The essay is also underdeveloped and disorganized. However, there are a number of good points. It contains relevant material such as the growing fear of Communism, the dissatisfaction of the middle classes, the surge of prosperity and industry in the 1920s, and the loss of wealth after the Wall Street Crash.

In 1932 5 million pepul wer out of work in Germany. Work-ers voted Comunist and the midul clres voted Nazi becos Hitler said he wud look af-ter shopkepers and formers.

Pepul in Germany started to look to the Nais after the Wall St Crash in 1929. Germany had been a welthy countree till then. They had recieved a loan from the US which helped them pay there reperation and set up Factories. In 1928 they did badly in the elections and got only 12 seats. Because of the Crash Factorys shut.

The midul clres wer scared of the Comnists.

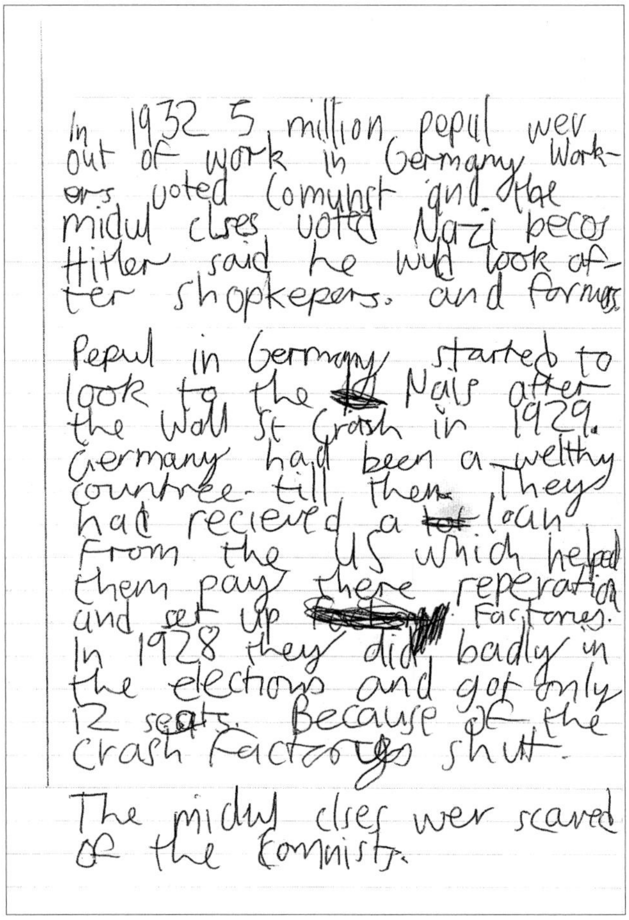

The answer needs reorganizing, points need developing and some basic spellings need to be learned, such as 'would', 'people', 'middle', 'factories', 'classes' and 'wealthy'. There is also some essential subject vocabulary such as 'Nazi', 'Communist' and 'reparations', which will never appear on a drill and practice spelling programme but that need to be mastered.

Spell checking

The use of a word processor makes the text legible and offers opportunities for different approaches to spelling. Matthew could use a spell checker by looking at each word that is underlined, right clicking the mouse and looking at alternatives, but there is a danger that he will accept suggestions for corrections without learning anything. Some children see common words corrected so frequently that they learn the correct spelling subconsciously; others become aware, perhaps for the

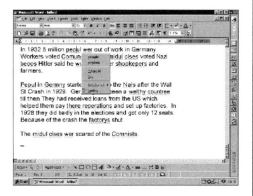

first time, that they have a particular problem with words and consciously register the correct spelling and make an effort the next time they want to use that word.

Track Changes

Another strategy is to use the *Track Changes* facility. This is in the *Tools* menu (Tools, Track Changes, Highlight Changes). Be sure to click on the Track Changes While Editing box. This facility records each change by crossing out text and substituting new words. When used in conjunction with the spell checker, it gives you a handy spelling list. The only two items the spell checker did not cope with were 'there', 'their' and the word 'Nazis'. Matthew now has a set of spellings to work on and learn.

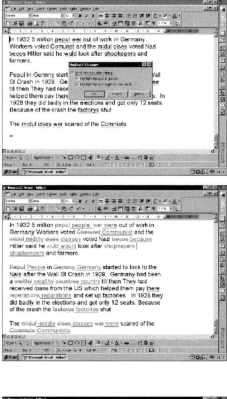

Using AutoCorrect and abbreviations

Some teachers and pupils may decide to speed up the writing process by using AutoCorrect to expand short forms of words. Many of us use abbreviations when we take notes – 'gov' for 'government', 'dev' for 'develop'. In this example, the pupil could put longer words on AutoCorrect. Alternatively, if Matthew is making extensive use of word processing for all subjects, he may start to use a wider range of abbreviations, e.g.

'wd' becomes 'would', 'shd' becomes 'should', to speed up his recording.

Some people see this as cheating, and worry that if the child is not laboriously writing out the words he will never learn to spell. However, writing is more than spelling and in this case Matthew needs to write a history essay. The spelling is important but he needs to marshal ideas, produce a coherent and relevant account, be able to understand the significance of different events and justify his opinions. To this end, if the corrections on this work focus only on spelling then it becomes an English lesson and not a history task. No teacher or parent should ever lose sight of the fact that writing is much more than spelling, whatever the child's ability.

- **Dictation software**, also known as voice recognition, allows the child to speak to the machine. This type of software is getting better, but the child will need a lot of training to use it effectively. Ideally it needs to be used with software that can read back what the machine thinks the child has said.

Dictation software in practice

Sean is a Year 10 student with dyslexia. Since he started at secondary school he has needed an amanuensis for nearly every important piece of written work. He loved the idea of speech recognition and was willing to put in the time to train the software.

He was able to speak consistently, if not always clearly. His one distinct advantage over other students was his ability to dictate. He had been used to dictating to an amanuensis for a number of years and the skills he developed were invaluable to him as he gained confidence with using the software. He was soon able to work independently; although he still experiences difficulties choosing the right words for correction, he is now able to produce text on his own for the first time ever.

- Some software can work with existing word processor programs and predicts what word the child is going to enter. An example of this is **Penfriend**.

  Penfriend opens up a small window that floats over the main program window. As a few letters are typed a list appears in the floating window of words that the program thinks you are going to type. Each choice is listed along with the function key (*F1* to *F12*) that you can press to complete the word. This makes typing much quicker for inexperienced typists. A useful feature is that it will speak out each letter as it is typed or the word if the function key is pressed. Once a full stop is reached the whole sentence is read out. If a block of text is highlighted it will read it all out for the pupil.

Available from Penfriend Ltd, 30 South Oswald Road, Edinburgh EH9 2HG.

Penfriend in practice

Martin is at school in the north-east. His teacher Alison sent this report:

Martin has a chronic inability to learn and retain literacy skills. His verbal skills are age-appropriate but his reading and writing are Level 1.

By 13 years of age, Martin had undergone a battery of approaches to develop his basic literacy skills; many of these approaches had been multi-sensory, including the Units of Sound recommended by the Dyslexia Institute. He had made some progress but he no longer had confidence in his chances of improving and accepted that he would never be able to read even the most regular of words consistently, nor produce written work intelligible to either himself or others.

He had been using *Penfriend* occasionally when word processing in class. He was encouraged to use his laptop consistently whenever he was to produce written work. He used the predictor window of *Penfriend*, sounding out options as he typed in the initial sounds. Because he used the incremental phonic approach to spellings, he was usually able to type in the correct initial sounds for most of his words. There were still some amusing errors as English threw up the usual anomalies but Martin found that he was producing work that made sense and that could be understood by others. This provided him with motivation to continue.

Now 15 and in Year 11, Martin is still unable to retain digraphs and regular letter combinations and so has to decode every word he reads, but his confidence is such that he has a degree of functional reading. His writing is generally intelligible with a reasonable attempt at longer irregular words. Martin has acquired strategies both with his laptop and without it to overcome some of his specific difficulties, sufficient to enable him to continue learning.

- Some teachers prefer to analyse the learner's error patterns and then create a range of tailor-made exercises using programs such as *GAMZ WordSearch* from Inclusive Technology, SPA's *WordSquare Maker* or *Taskmagic* (http://www.mdlsoft.co.uk). You can set up a word list and the computer will generate a puzzle on the screen that can be solved on-screen or printed out to use away from the computer. Topics might include science terms, vocabulary for geography or names of characters from play or novel.
- **Software to support vocabulary and syntax.** Programs such as *Clicker* or *Word Bar* are useful for support and over-learning. They can help with vocabulary as well as spelling. Each word can be typed into a separate cell, with its definition or personal notes to jog the memory about how to spell it. Learners can scan through the grids to revise spellings or click in the cell to enter the word straight into their written work. Left clicking

Try to solve this puzzle.

```
K C A J M A C S R S C A B L B
C H V E Z I K S O Z K D R E S
V O T S O C K S V X X R I K S
J E A I L G L O W S H I R T O
G A J T E F P Y J A M K J J S
F P C W A E J S C S A B U E T
X Y A K L J Y P O G H W H A R
I J U V E H·R T W L Z O V N O
W A I U B T W G E O B D E S U
G M X N L S W H V V X N S S S
F A T E O C I L Q E T S T N E
W S L O U A H U C S H K N T R
D H A T S R R T V I W I O X S
V E C I E F V O K L G R W S H
V D R E S S T J E A I T M J E
```

Here are the words...

BLOUSE	DRESS	GLOVES	HAT
JACKET	JEANS	SCARF	SHIRT
SKIRT	SOCKS	SHOES	TIE
TROUSERS	COAT	VEST	PYJAMAS

on the cell lets them hear the word so they can double-check to make sure they have picked out the word they really want.

- Text disclosure programs such as *Developing Tray,* and programs using cloze procedure such as *Cloze* from Crick software can be used to develop syntax as pupils engage with different styles of writing. The teacher types in a text containing a number of target words and saves the exercise. The file can then be opened and displayed on the screen as a series of blanks, waiting to be filled in. The teacher fills in some of the text, leaving only the key words blank. This is saved as a partly completed text. When the learner loads the text, only the target words need to be uncovered.

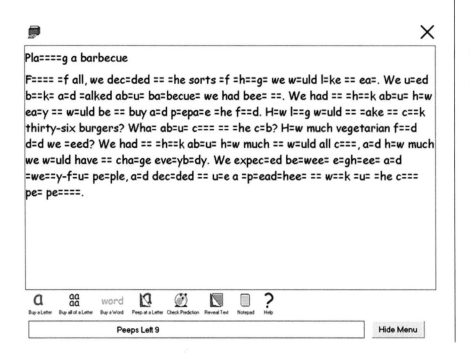

Supporting Children

Using ICT to overcome particular problems

ICT can also help pupils to overcome some of their particular problems when accessing learning materials.

Working with printed text

ICT can be used to make printed text more accessible. Pupils can scan printed text from a book into a word-processing package and have it read out to them.

> Jack was very frustrated as he had problems decoding the words in his textbook, working out which bits he wanted and copying them into an exercise book. He kept losing his place and could not make sense of what he was reading. He learned to use a scanner to put the text into Word and then got the computer to read the text to him. Once everything was together on screen, all he had to do was delete the bits he did not need. He had a framework to build on.

For individual words in a book, you might try a scanning pen such as the Oxford Reading Pen *11* (Quicktionary). You run the nib over a word and the pen will read it out loud over a loudspeaker or through an earphone. It will also show you how to break the word into syllables and give you a definition. You must practise to get the angle and speed right or it can be frustrating. (Visit http://www.wizcom.co.il.)

Working with on-screen text

It is possible to make the text in web pages bigger and easier to read and to change the colour of 'paper' and text to combinations that suit an individual user's needs. If black print on a white background is proving a problem, change the colours and font on your computer. Right click on an empty area on the desktop. This will bring up a menu; click on *Properties* to open up the *Display Properties* window. Click on the *Appearance* tab and choose *Colour scheme.* You can now choose different schemes that can be used for the desktop and most applications. Many people like turquoise, cream or pale grey. This is less of a contrast than black text on a white background and is easier to read.

In many schools technicians do not let users change settings and many do not allow for individual user profiles, but this will have to change as the Disability Discrimination Act begins to make more of an impact. At present one easy way of making sure pupils have the right colour combinations for word processing each time is to teach them to set up colours in Word. Go to the *View* menu and choose *Web.* Then go to *Format – Background* and choose a colour for the 'paper'. To choose the colour of the text go to *Format – Font* and pick a colour.

One major problem for learners is getting hold of information and putting ideas into their own words so that they have some content to work with. These days, many pupils will be looking for information on the Internet as it is up to date, often has pictures, videos, animations or other multimedia features that make it more appealing and accessible to learners who struggle with print. Teach pupils to go to *View – Text Size* and make the print bigger.

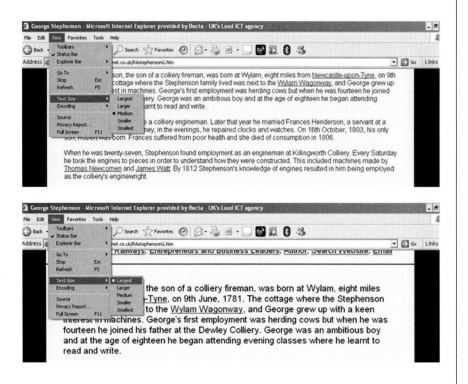

Medium text

Large text

There are also specialist programs to help pupils read web pages. *ReadAble* from Iansyst manages your computer's colour and font settings. It can be set up to change the default text colour, the menu background and text colour and the toolbars in *Word* and for web pages.

Communicate Web wide from Widgit software can separate out text and pictures in web pages, make the font bigger and increase the spacing between lines to make the page easier to read for those with poor scanning skills.

Claro Read and WordRead from http://www.clarosoftware.com offer a range of facilities for dyslexic readers. *WordRead*, which you can trial for free from http://www.clarosoftware.com, is a toolbar that sits on top of your documents, emails or Internet and will read out the text. It also has an audio facility to read back text using a real voice. You can listen to *Word* documents, emails, spreadsheets, *PowerPoint* presentations, web pages and some PDF files. You can make audio files of complete documents or articles and listen to them on an audio player or on your computer.

Claro Read can read back menus, button texts and tool tips, as well as any text displayed on the screen

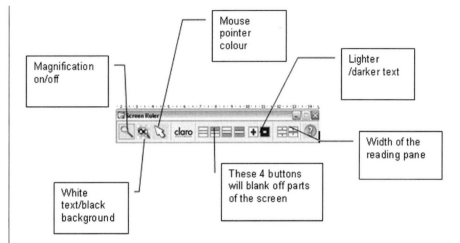

ClaroRead PLUS version will also echo back text dictated using Dragon NaturallySpeaking speech recognition software. It offers OCR (optical character recognition) so pupils can scan in passages from a textbook, change font, colours, text size, as well as the spacing between characters, lines and paragraphs. It also can be used for composing text and has word prediction.

Screen Ruler is a visual tracking aid. This provides a 'strip' or 'ruler' across the screen. Text inside the strip will be magnified, or can have the contrast changed and the background 'greyed' or 'dimmed' out. *ScreenRuler* will work with any piece of software, as it acts as an 'overlay' on the PC screen.

what Dominique has been through.

Each week, she has a meeting with her, where they discuss any problems she is having - from claiming

nutritious food, and identifying and pursuing training or work opportunities. Our aim is to give them all the tools they need to live independent and fulfilling lives.

Speech feedback

One of the most useful facilities a computer can offer is the use of speech feedback. Where short-term memory causes a child to forget the beginning of a sentence before they get to the end, a talking word processor can provide a prompt by reading back what has already been written. More modern packages offer a range of voices – male, female, child, robot. Some children who have been unwilling to commit their thoughts to paper enjoy the challenge of typing words for the computer to say. It is interesting to notice how many swear words are phonic and give children the chance to discover that double consonants shorten the vowel sound!

It can be really handy to take a document and convert it to a sound file, for example a literature text from the Project Gutenberg site – http://www.gutenberg.org/. If you want to play with converting text to speech and sound files, try *Natural Voice Reader*, which you can download free of charge from http://www.naturalreaders.com/download.htm.

Using speech in the classroom can be tricky and some learners do not like it. On the plus side, it can give access to text to poor readers and this makes them more independent. It frees up the teacher or learning support assistant to give more effective, specialist support instead of just being a reader. However, on the down side it can be noisy and distracting. It is a good idea – and indeed is policy in some schools – to encourage pupils to provide their own headphones because head lice thrive and multiply in the foam on the earpieces.

Research skills

Older readers use screen readers or talking word processors to access worksheets, emails and information from CD-ROM encyclopaedias and other resources.

Researching in practice

Robert was studying slavery for Key Stage 3 history. He enjoyed class discussions and the videos but was discouraged by the textbooks. He found it particularly hard to use an index since, by the time he had worked through the alphabet, found the heading, noted the page number and started looking for the entry, he had forgotten what he wanted to know! His teacher showed him how to use *Africana*. He had a go with the virtual tour of slave port and then found articles he wanted. He highlighted them and copied them into *Word*. He listened to the information and decided what he wanted to keep and what could be deleted. He spent a long time editing the document and produced a long and detailed piece of work that showed his enthusiasm and considerable knowledge.

Pupils with poor literacy skills often have problems knowing what to put into an essay and may be tempted to copy out large chunks from a book. In the past, they were limited by how tired their hand became but with the digital age, pupils can download great chunks of information from the Internet and present them as an essay. This will not help them to develop their skills in reading, writing or processing information.

Using the highlighter

One useful tool here is the highlighter. If you copy text into *Word* either from a web page or by scanning pages from a book, the highlighter lets you pick out the key features. This helps with reading for meaning, which can be a difficult skill for pupils who struggle to decode individual words. Look at this example.

Highlighter

Highlighter in practice

Rob had to read the text and pick out the facilities that might appeal to a British tourist. He found it hard because he is a poor reader who loses his place easily. His LSA copied the information into *Word* and changed the font to Comic Sans, which is a sans serif font with wide spacing between the lines. Rob found blue text on a blue background made his eyes less tired and he could read for longer. He used the highlighter to pick out points. This meant he could find them again very easily without having to re-read everything over and over again.

Rhodes is one of the largest and most popular of the Dodecanese Islands in Greece. It has 370km of coastline on the Mediterranean, which has resulted in the east coast of the island being lined with sandy beaches. Rhodes is most cosmopolitan islands and enjoys more sunshine than anywhere else in Greece. It is a big island and an excellent place to explore, with its mountainous views fabulous beaches and excellent attractions such as the Acropolis of Lindos and Valley of the Butterfly. Rhodes town is divided into two distinct and unequal parts - the old town contained within the walls of a medieval fortress and the the modern half with restaurants, chic hotels, clubs and fashionable shops sprawling round it in three directions, made up of tourist complexes, beaches and numerous hotels. Rhodes is a popular tourist destination due to its historical monuments and archaeological sites. There are good road and bus networks to and from most towns and villages on the island allowing it all to be explored relatively easily.

Insert Comment

Some teachers are using the *Insert Comment* facility on the *Insert* menu to develop digital marking. This is where the teacher's marking appears on the screen. This is particularly good for GCSE coursework where many rewrites are needed before the pupil produces a piece of work that accurately reflects his ability. For pupils with poor visual tracking skills, it is difficult to look at their work on-screen and then look down at a print-out with handwritten comments on it and then back to the right place on the screen to make changes. With digital marking, the teacher's comments are legible and are on-screen, close to the relevant piece of the essay.

The Spike

The Spike is a little-known but very useful facility in Word that lets the user select bits of information and put it on the clipboard. It's a bit like *Cut* and *Paste* but it allows you to gather up lots of information from different parts of a document and then paste them all at once.

It may be that you use the highlighter first to pick out the main points. Then run the cursor over each point in turn, pressing *Ctrl* and the *F3 key* to select the point. Keep going until you have all the points you want. The Spike will hold an almost indefinite amount of information. Then on a new document, press the *shift key, Ctrl* and the *F3 key* and it will paste all the material you have chosen.

In newer versions of Word, you can select up to 24 pieces of information, which appear separately in a window at the side of your document. This gives users greater control over the order in which they want to use the information.

the Depression.
used the Jews
as scapegoats
promised to make Germany proud again
Farmers
Higher prices for their produce – making up for all their
losses during the Depression.

Now Matthew has a set of notes he can expand or incorporate into his essay. Again everything is in one place, on-screen, and he is focusing on the writing task and not searching endlessly through books or notes or struggling with an index to find the page he wants. With the computer, he is in control and has an increasing range of strategies at his command in his quest to become an independent writer.

ICT in practice

For teachers of learners with dyslexia there is a desire to find a method of 'over-learning' spelling and reading patterns that will succeed where traditional classroom methods have failed. Often teachers see the computer as the natural solution to this problem. Certainly for the child with short-term memory or attention problems the computer can be a regular prompter and incentive to stay on task.

Over the years a large number of packages have come on to the market that have been developed to reinforce particular teaching points. The question is, how suitable will they be for any individual learner? The criteria listed below provide a starting point:

- **Can the speed of presentation and response be altered?** A program that flashes information on to the screen too quickly or requires a reaction beyond the capabilities of the learner will encourage guessing instead of a considered response; a program that moves too slowly will result in poor concentration. A long introduction is useful first time around, but becomes boring once you know it too well.
- **Is the display clear?** For learners who have problems with information processing, a cluttered screen with distracting colours and movement can hinder understanding.
- **Can the length of the game be altered?** A good game will allow the teacher to decide the number of goes or the success rate to be achieved for successful completion.
- **Can the sound level be altered?** A nasty noise that broadcasts the fact that you have made an error is not helpful for some learners.
- **Does the program save the settings?** It is a boon in a busy schedule if next time you come to the program you can continue with the same options.
- **Does the program encourage the learner to work independently?** Is the task clear? Will the learner need to read on-screen instructions in order to tackle the required task? Are essential instructions spoken and/or can they be read by a screen reader if needed?

The teacher chose a program for Hugh, with target words within his reading level. The on-screen instructions and sentences surrounding the target words were too advanced, leaving Hugh unable to work independently.

- **Can word lists be edited?** A good program will allow the teacher to enter word lists designed to support the learner's learning and to include subject-specific vocabulary.
- **What happens when the learner makes a mistake?** There is nothing worse than getting caught in a loop where the software will not continue unless you get the answer right but provides no help if you get it wrong.
- **Does it use rewards and penalties?**

James, Year 6, loved playing a spelling game where if he got the word wrong a little man would appear on-screen, pick up the word, screw it up and throw it into a dustbin. Unfortunately James found it more fun to get the word wrong!

Here the penalties were more attractive than the rewards and got in the way of learning.

Improving access to the curriculum

It is sometimes assumed that dyslexia affects literacy and that the impact will be felt mainly in subjects that require a lot of reading and essay writing. This is not always the case. Dyscalculia – the impact of specific learning difficulties on mathematics and numeracy – is dealt with in a separate chapter. However, the subject specialist in secondary school needs to be aware of problems that might arise in their subject area and have some strategies in place to deal with them.

Subject	Skills	Ideas for dyslexic learners
Art	Measuring, recording, perspective	Writing frames for art journal, encourage use of sketches for planning
D&T	Measuring, recording	Practise measurement and double-check it! provide lists of terminology for measurement, rules, formulae
English	Reading and recalling texts, e.g. Shakespeare Creating different styles of writing Spelling Grammar	Try multimedia versions, e.g. Don Johnston *Start to Finish Romeo and Juliet, Macbeth* http://www.donjohnston.co.uk/ Kar2ouche *Twelfth Night* http://www.immersiveeducation.com/ Use tapes, videos, lots of activities analysing and interaction with text Electronic texts http://www.gutenberg.org/ Working with writing frames
Geography	Reading maps, visualizing terrain from maps, producing work that shows analysis and explanation and not just recall	Working with writing frames, Google maps http://maps.google.co.uk/ Matching maps with satellite images
History	Recall, sequencing, producing work that shows analysis and explanation and not just recall	Working with writing frames
MFL	Left and right, numbers, money, telling the time, spelling	Use spell checker in target language; use talking word processing package such as *Textease*, http://www.softease.com/ Provide lots of activities for over-learning and reinforcement
Mathematics	Estimation, getting meaning from graphs, poor understanding of statistics and ratio	See Chapter 6

Impact of dyslexia on different subjects

Subject	Skills	Ideas for dyslexic learners
Science	Sequencing, remembering and recalling instructions	Pair with a buddy for experiments; provide examples of what good work looks like. Pair with a buddy for some write-ups
PE	Following sequence, left and right, may have some clumsiness too	Pair with a buddy

Summary

- Technology can be highly motivating.
- Word processing makes work legible and attractive.
- Spell checkers, voice recognition and predictive word processors can revolutionize writing.
- It's worth considering specialist software to improve visual and auditory memory, and programs to help with planning.
- There are specific drill and practice programs to help with spelling.
- Alternatively you can use framework software to improve word recognition and syntax.
- When producing an extended piece of work it is worth looking at the tools.
- Curriculum specialists need to support dyslexic learners in their subject.
- Changing the colours and fonts, especially in Word, can make text more readable.
- Changing text size for web pages makes information easier to read.
- Specialist software can change the appearance of text and read back information to the learner.
- Talking word processors can make learners more independent and free up teacher time.
- Pupils need to be trained to skim, scan and make notes. Using the highlighter tool can help.
- Use the *Track Changes* facility in conjunction with the spell checker to produce a spelling list.
- Speed up the writing process by using *AutoCorrect* to expand short forms of words.
- Develop digital marking, which is especially useful for pupils with poor visual tracking skills.
- Use the *Spike* or the clipboard to collect all the points you need from a text and then paste them as a set of notes or a plan.

5 | Organization and Planning Skills

General organization

We often take it for granted that children will arrive on time to lessons with all the things that they need. But this requires a high degree of skill, planning and organization. Some dyslexic pupils develop a simple compensatory strategy – they carry everything with them for the whole week!

Parents can help by encouraging their child to develop good habits. They can:

- have a lesson and homework timetable visible at home and check it each night as their child arrives home from school (see page 96);
- establish a routine for homework – before/after tea, before school in the morning – and check that it has been completed;
- help their child to prioritize homework tasks – what needs doing for tomorrow, what can be left until the weekend (without creating a huge backlog!);
- help their child to get into the habit of preparing and packing his school-bag ready for the next day;
- provide plastic wallets or envelope files for letters to and from school to increase the chances of messages being passed on correctly;
- provide a case for pencils, pens and rulers and have a good stock of spares at home to replace those lost or mislaid during the day;
- regularly check that the homework diary is being used and kept up to date.

Teachers can help by:

- Having spare equipment that the pupil can borrow for the duration of the lesson if they have lost theirs. This should be done without fuss.
- Prompting the child to take out necessary equipment and homework at the start of the lesson. Some teachers have this as an expectation for the whole class and encourage it through praise.
- Writing important messages for parents in a home-school book. Some dyslexic children have poor memories and even if they remember there is something to tell their parents, they might not remember what it is.

Sunday	Monday	Tuesday	Wednesday	Thursday	Friday	Saturday
	1	1	1	1	1	
	2	2	2	2	2	
	3	3	3	3	3	
	4	4	4	4	4	
	5	5	5	5	5	
	At home	At home	At home	At home	At home	
Pack swimming kit	Do homework for:	Do homework for:	Do homework for:	Do homework for:	Do homework for:	Make sure all sports kit and school uniform is washed
Check that all homework is done	Pack PE kit	Pack PE kit	Collect materials for D+T	Pack Karate kit	Pack PE kit	
Dinner money						
Bus fare/pass						

- Writing homework into the child's planner or asking a more competent peer to check that the child has written it down correctly, or providing a typed sheet.
- Making it clear when work must be handed in.
- Providing additional copies of timetables and school plans to increase the number of reference points for the child and take into account that they may not be organized enough to keep a single copy with them at all times. Copies could be stuck into planners, put in their bedroom, on the fridge, on the form room notice board, in their locker, etc.
- Regularly checking that the homework diary or planner is being used and kept up to date.

Extended writing

For a dyslexic child, the idea of attempting a large piece of independent writing can be daunting. Emotionally the task can seem impossible. Organizationally, it may result in an almost random presentation of ideas. Extended writing requires an element of planning and organization. At the simplest level, this requires that the piece of work has a clear beginning, middle and end.

The teacher can support the child by providing the structure in the form of a writing frame. This breaks the overall task down into smaller sub-tasks, each with a clear indication of what is needed in each section. It also provides easy checkpoints for the teacher and pupil to review how the task is going.

Planning of extended writing can, and should, be taught. One method is to brainstorm, then use spider diagrams or mind-maps to record ideas quickly. The ideas are then sequenced to produce the order in which they could be written. The next step is to write a rough draft for each idea. These are then written together with joining phrases (and signposts). Finally, the draft is read and adjusted to produce the final piece of work. This process can be modelled by the teacher and teaching assistant, with regular practice of each stage until the pupil is familiar with the process. An aide-mémoire can be useful to keep pupils on task (see page 98).

Revision and coursework planning

Learning material for an examination requires a number of skills. Basic facts have to be memorized, processes have to be learned and skills mastered. Previous examination papers can be used as a source of questions to allow the skills to be practised. The danger is that the child does not allow enough time to cover the entire syllabus or focuses too much on one area at the expense of the others.

Writing essays and assignments

This piece of work is about: ....

In doing the work I need to: (find out/explore/decide/describe/consider/argue/discuss/comment on/evaluate/summarize)

....

....

The work should be about.....................................words/pages long.

The work should be hand written/word processed.

It must be handed in on ....

Before starting to write:

1. Do I understand what I have to do? (If not, ask your teacher, teaching assistant and/or a classmate.)
2. Have I got all the information I need? (Lesson notes, textbook, library books, information from the Internet or from talking to other people.)
3. Make a list of your ideas/thoughts/facts/observations. Then make short notes on each one, using your own words to show your understanding. Leave plenty of space around your notes for extra thoughts, inserting 'better' words, etc. Put these points in a logical order.

When writing:

1. Introduce your work with a sentence or paragraph explaining what you are setting out to do.
2. Open each new paragraph with a clear explanation/statement/observation then use evidence or further information to 'flesh out' your ideas.
3. Finish with a closing paragraph that summarizes what you have found out or what you think.

After writing:

1. Read through your work and check that:
   - it makes sense;
   - it uses an appropriate 'voice' for the task/audience;
   - it answers the question/addresses the topic;
   - punctuation and spelling are correct.
2. Ask yourself – 'Have I missed anything out? Is there anything I could do to make it better?'

It is always worth asking a friend or parent to read your work before handing it in – sometimes they can see something that is quite obvious to the reader, but not at all obvious to the writer (this is the case with very accomplished writers too!).

Similar problems exist for coursework. Information has to be sought out, structured and then presented. Coursework usually has to be completed by set deadlines and for a whole range of subjects. At the start of a GCSE course these deadlines can seem a long way off and the child may do nothing during the early stages, only to have a mad rush at the end of the course.

Parents and teachers can support the child by:

- making a timetable for doing different activities and subjects;
- devising a simple project planner that breaks down the overall task and sets mini-deadlines to complete set pieces of the project;
- reviewing progress frequently (half-termly or more often if necessary);
- helping to keep different subject files organized so that time is used more efficiently and important information or work does not get muddled up or lost.

It is also important to be realistic about how much information can be 'crammed' during revision. Help the child by looking through past examination papers to divide the content into three areas:

- essential
- important
- useful 'if there is time'.

Metacognitive strategies are those that involve the pupil thinking about the study skills needed and how to develop them most effectively:

- What helps him to learn?
- What hinders him?

Consideration of preferred learning styles can be helpful:

- Are visual representations easier to 'fix' (e.g. mind-maps)?
- Does colour help?
- Does listening to explanations/texts help – would tape recordings be useful?

If the pupil has to explain something to someone (a brother, sister, parent or grandparent) it may help him to understand and remember it better. Revision should consist of more than simply reading through notes and will be most effective when:

- it is active, e.g. converting notes from one form to another, changing written notes to mind-maps, producing question and answer cards, copying diagrams and labelling them from memory;
- it is involved in creating meaning, e.g. using information to answer model questions;
- study periods are short but frequent.

Examination vocabulary

Teach children how to read common words used in examinations and explain what they mean. Build up the child's vocabulary by going through past papers and identifying examination words and common sentence structures. Poor readers are often thrown by words that are not difficult to read but carry very little information. For example:

'Solve 6+3'

The pupil may be very capable of working out the sum, but be completely thrown by the word 'solve'. As they progress through school, there is an ever-growing list of vocabulary that pupils need to be able to read and understand. A checklist is provided on pages 102 and 103 with spaces for the teacher or pupil to add definitions.

Special examination conditions

In cases of more severe dyslexia, it may be possible to apply for special conditions within the exam itself. This may be an extra time allowance for the pupil, use of a word processor, a reader or an amanuensis (a scribe). This usually requires a written request and an assessment report from an Educational Psychologist or appropriately qualified teacher. Assessment reports are only valid for two years. This is because the pupil may have improved and this would give an unfair advantage.

Teachers who have a recognized qualification in dyslexia or psychology can conduct an educational assessment. The examination boards have published a list of acceptable qualifications. This maintains an appropriate level of quality control. It ensures that candidates are not unfairly disadvantaged, nor are they given an unfair advantage.

A complete list of qualifications that are accepted by the examination boards can be obtained from the Examination Board websites. This list is updated each year as more courses are accredited. Teachers can also take a brief course that leads to a Certificate of Competence in Educational Testing (Level A) accredited by the British Psychological Society. More details can be found on the BPS website at http://www.psychtesting.org.uk

Schools wanting to make special arrangements for pupils in SATs must notify an LEA representative who monitors the situation. Non-LEA schools should contact QCA. An Educational Psychologist's assessment is not needed for special arrangements for these tests.

Examination Boards for GCSE, GCE 'A' levels and GNVQ examinations will require a current assessment report from an Educational Psychologist or from a teacher with specialist qualifications for identi-

Copies of the booklets:
- *Key Stage 1 Assessment and reporting arrangements*
- *Key Stage 2 Assessment and reporting arrangements*
- *Key Stage 3 Assessment and reporting arrangements*
are available free of charge from the Qualifications and Curriculum Authority (QCA)
Tel: 01787 884 444;
Fax: 01787 312 950;
Email: info@qca.org.uk
and www.qca.org.uk

Supporting Children

GCE, VCE, GCSE &
GNVQ Regulations
and Guidance
relating to Candidates
with Particular
Requirements.
*Issued by the Joint
Council for General
Qualifications.
Available from the
awarding bodies
including:*
- *Assessment &
  Qualification Alliance
  (AQA) Manchester;
  Tel: 0161 953 1180*
- *Assessment &
  Qualification Alliance
  (AQA) Guildford;
  Tel: 01483 506 506*

**Examination Board
websites**
- *Assessment and
  Qualifications
  Alliance (AEB,
  SEG and NEAB):
  www.aqa.org.uk*
- *Edexcel:
  www.edexcel.org.uk*
- *OCR: www.ocr.org.uk*
- *Northern
  Ireland Council
  for Curriculum
  Examinations
  and Assessment:
  www.cea.org.uk*
- *Welsh Joint Education
  Committee:
  www.wjec.co.uk*

fying, assessing and teaching pupils with dyslexia. Schools may be required to pay LEAs for such assessments. The report may not have to be submitted, but must be available if required.

Summary

Organization and planning skills can be supported by:

- parents helping to develop good habits and supportive routines
- teachers helping with general organization
- teaching essay writing and thinking skills before writing starts
- considering how to revise and plan coursework
- learning the words used by examiners
- asking for special examination conditions.

Examination wordlist

Word	What does it mean?
Accurate	....
Analyse/analysis	....
Approximate	....
Categorize	....
Cause (and effect)	....
Characteristic	....
Comment	....
Compare	....
Consider	....
Contrast	....
Critical/criticize	....
Data	....
Decide	....
Deduce	....
Define	....
Discuss	....
Distinguish	....
Effect	....
Essential	....
Evaluate	....
Examine	....
Extent	....

Factor ....

Function ....
....

Hypothesis/hypothesize ....
....

Illustrate ....
....

Interpret ....
....

Justify ....
....

Maximum ....
....

Minimum ....
....

Optimal ....
....

Organize ....
....

Outline ....
....

Predict ....
....

Process ....
....

Prove ....
....

Purpose ....
....

Reason ....
....

Relate ....
....

Review ....
....

State ....
....

Summarize ....
....

Synthesis/synthesize ....
....

6 | Dyslexia and Dyscalculia

Just over half of dyslexic children have difficulty with mathematics and with number concepts (BDA, 2001). Some children who can read and spell adequately also seem to have a difficulty with number. Dyscalculia is a term that refers to a specific learning difficulty in the area of number or mathematics. Ta'ir et al. (1997) define it as 'a cognitive disorder of childhood affecting the ability of an otherwise intelligent child to learn arithmetic'. The Questions Publishing guide (2004) differentiates between a less severe form defined by a discrepancy between attainment in mathematics and predicted attainment and a more severe form where there is a complete inability to grasp mathematical concepts. Severe dyscalculia is sometimes referred to as acalculia. Dyscalculia can be a feature of childhood and failure to learn numerical concepts in school and is referred to as developmental dyscalculia or it can result from injury or brain disease in adulthood and is then referred to as acquired dyscalculia.

There is some evidence to suggest that developmental dyscalculia is a brain-based disorder with a genetic predisposition (Shalev and Gross-Tsur, 2001). The role of teaching cannot be ignored and some writers cite an increase in children with dyscalculia as being a consequence of teaching non-negotiable targets set in the National Numeracy Strategy (Henderson and Chinn, 2004). Estimates of the number of dyscalculiac children suggest that it is a high-incidence disorder affecting about 3–6% of the school population (Braundet et al., 2004; McCrone, 2002; Shalev and Gross-Tsur, 2001). The DfES is responding to this with suggestions for Wave 3 interventions in numeracy (Gross, 2004).

Learners may experience difficulties with all or some of the following areas:

- conservation of number
- counting
- number recognition
- place value
- attaching meaning to symbols
- the language of mathematics
- recognizing patterns.

While dyslexia has been recognized for many years this is not the case for dyscalculia. There is very little research to help us understand dyscalculia, though some is starting to emerge. Literacy has formed the main push for education and for special educational needs, partly because the delivery of the rest of the curriculum is dependent on text and partly because of the recognized need for adults to be literate. A difficulty with number has only recently started to attract the same level of attention with the introduction of the National Numeracy Strategy. This means that there is much debate to be held before a clear consensus and working practice will emerge. In many ways the debate over dyscalculia is just at the point that the debate for dyslexia was at 30 years ago. An editorial comment in *The Lancet* reflects this to some extent:

> *If you have not heard about dyscalculia, you soon will, it is becoming a highly fashionable diagnosis for kids that struggle with their maths.*
> (McCrone, 2002)

As with dyslexia, the definition of dyscalculia suffers from a number of difficulties:

- **Defining the extent of difficulty required to be considered as dyscalculia** rather than just having a weakness in number. How bad do you have to be before you become acalculiac? What level of difficulty with number leads to dysfunction in adulthood? What level of skill is expected in number for children of different ages anyway?
- **Differentiating between dyscalculia and other causes of poor performance** (e.g. poor teaching, learned helplessness, emotional blocking, mathematical anxiety, general learning difficulties, environmental deprivation). How likely is it that remedial teaching using structured programmes will overcome the difficulty and help the child catch up with peers? Are there underlying concepts or skills that must be secure before higher-level concepts and skills are taught? At what stage is it necessary to teach coping strategies to mitigate the difficulties?
- **Differentiating between dyscalculia and other conditions.** Is it really different from dyslexia? Could difficulties in sequencing numerical operations be caused by dyspraxia? What do other syndromes tell us about dyscalculia?
- **Determining precisely what the nature of the difficulty is** (is it about quantity or is it about procedures or is it about symbols?).
- **Explaining the causation.**
- **Finding the appropriate strategies for remediation, mitigation and inclusion.**

Degree of difficulty

Shalev and Gross-Tsur (2001) argue that 9-year-old children are dyscalculiac if they can perform simple counting skills, can handle money, understand dates and time but cannot retrieve over-learned numerical information or have to resort to inefficient strategies to solve numerical problems. This level of skill development does not seem as severe as that highlighted by other researchers. For example,

Garty *et al.* (1989) provide a case study of a 12-year-old boy who had great difficulty with Grade 2 arithmetic. The variation in degree of difficulty needed is described in Landerl *et al.* (2004) and ranges from 35th centile by Geary and colleagues down to the 11th centile used by the Buterworth Dyscalculiac Screener. Even this lower number is way above the estimates of prevalence and may be over-inclusive in its diagnosis of dyscalculia.

Clearly the age of the child and the expected levels of attainment are going to be important in deciding whether the dyscalculiac label is used. However, we could talk about functional levels of skill instead. The DSM-IV definition includes the idea that the child must experience disruption to academic achievement or daily living (Landerl *et al.*, 2004). How much number knowledge or mathematical knowledge do you need to be able to function as a 'normal' adult (rather than one who requires special number skills for their job)? The exact level of skill is debatable. Perhaps we need to be able to:

- know how much money we have, how much change to expect from a shop and how to compare prices in different shops;
- know how to tell the time and understand dates;
- be able to recognize how many items we have, identify when we have one missing or when we have more than we need;
- be able to do simple divisions (say dividing by 4 family members), and so on.

The Basic Skills Agency published a report which shows that poor numeracy skills can be a serious obstacle hindrance to getting and keeping a job. Data in a second report (BSA, 2000) gives some idea of the level of skill held by adults:

- Calculate change expected in   80% abstract   88% with coins
  a shop
- Use a timetable   68%–72%
- Calculate floor space   71%
- Read a graph   92%
- Do simple multiplication using   98%
  pictures
- Apply multiplication and   89%
  addition to money
- Apply division to problem   76%
- Work out value for money   62%
- Understand interest-rate tables   74%
- Calculate multistep problems   31%
- Extract information from graph   96%

The majority of adults cannot perform multistep numerical problems and this normative effect may be why people will proudly say that they are not good at mathematics but would be ashamed to say that they cannot read.

Normal development of number skills

The ability to learn about numbers seems to be innate. Neonatal studies with 1-week old babies have shown that they are sensitive to the changes in the number of things. Although they cannot tell us directly what they have noticed we know that babies will look longer at something that they do not understand. They will look longer at a display where the number of items changes than a display where items are substituted but the number remains the same. In a second study, babies were sat in front of a screen. A doll was placed behind the screen, a second doll was shown to the baby and also placed behind the screen – but surreptitiously removed by the researcher. Once the screen was removed the babies looked a lot longer than when the researcher did not remove the second doll. This suggests that they had done some simple arithmetic and were expecting to see two dolls (1+1=2). Theories about how 'normal' children develop numerical ability beyond this point can help us to understand what might be going wrong for children who have dyscalculia.

Three approaches have influenced the study of children's number development (Ta'ir et al., 1997):

- Piaget's idea that children go through certain developmental stages in which certain logical principles appear. The child cannot be taught these principles until they have the mental capacity to grasp them. This theory would predict that a delay in the development of arithmetical skills would be accompanied by a similar delay in other cognitive areas.
- Fodor and Gelman also suggest that development happens across many domains in unison. However, they propose that the acquisition of knowledge is dependent on specific innate mechanisms (e.g. the language acquisition device proposed by Chomsky). This theory would allow for the possibility of a specific impairment in one of the innate mechanisms that could lead to a failure to develop in one domain (e.g. arithmetic skills).
- Vygotsky suggests that the interaction between the child's intellectual capacity and culture is important. It is the child's experience of learning in the social world in which a more competent (teacher) scaffolds learning experiences so that the child operates in the zone of proximal development. A child who does not receive good quality teaching at the right level will not acquire mathematical skills. Equally, a child with a specific cognitive impairment in mathematics will not benefit from an intensive programme to teach mathematical skills.

Age	Examples of number skills
3 to 4 years	Can count 3 or 4 bricks arranged in a line (touching each one in relational counting). Can count by rote from 1 to 5.
5 years	Can count up to 15 items. Counts objects in sequence (with one-to-one correspondence). The concept of quantity lags behind number sequencing ability. Conservation of number and volume has not been acquired. The child is cognitively at the Piagetian pre-operational stage.
6 years	Concrete operations stage of development is reached for most children between the ages of 6 and 8. This means that conservation has been acquired and problems can be solved in practical formats. Can name some numerals. Many 6-year-old children will reverse digits when writing. One-third will reverse numbers when writing single integers (O'Hare *et al.*, 1991).
8 years	Children can learn to recognize and write operational signs without necessarily knowing how to use them.
9 to 12 years	Children become proficient at all four rules of number. Dyscalculia is characterized by incomplete procedural knowledge and inefficient strategies to solve numerical problems (Shalev and Gross-Tsur, 2001).

The National Numeracy Strategy is a teaching scheme that aims to introduce naive children into the social and cultural aspects of mathematics used by adults. It does provide a hierarchical framework for teaching numeracy. It does not start from the basis of what children would be expected to do at different developmental stages. It does not ensure that children have mastered concepts before moving on to the next element of teaching. In this respect it is curriculum-led teaching and assumes that all children will learn at the same pace. Failure to acquire numerical understanding is dealt with through provision of the Springboard small-group booster lessons – these are also curriculum led, having a set programme of content to be delivered in a set timescale. It is only when the curriculum-led approach has failed some children that a child-led model can be used to support teaching using Wave 3 interventions. Some children may appear to be dyscalculiac but this is simply a feature of a curriculum-led approach to teaching. Good remedial teaching that takes the child's cognitive development and previous learning of skills into account will resolve these difficulties. For a few children, even this will not help – these are the children who are truly dyscalculiac.

Nature of dyscalculia

While there is disagreement about the nature of dyscalculia it is useful to consider the features that some authors cite:

- Difficulties with quantities. Does the child know that one more item has been added to a group? Can they tell that one pile has more items than another? Can they conserve number? Can they subitize (know how many items are present without counting)?
- Sequencing difficulties when reading or writing numbers, e.g. does the child read 721 as 712?
- Does the child know the relative size of different numbers (e.g. 10 is bigger than 5, a hundred is smaller than a thousand)? Can they deal with decimals and fractions?
- Can the child carry out the different mathematical processes involved in the four rules of number?
- Working memory difficulties that limit how much information can be held in mind while completing numerical operations. Can the child allocate attention to holding a subtotal in working memory, while also remembering the numbers being worked with and the steps involved in completing the problem success-fully? Does their performance at mental mathematics fall below their performance when they are allowed to use paper to help them extend working memory?
- Language difficulties. Can the child name numbers? Can they use mathematical concepts such as bigger, smaller, add, first, last? Do they know all the different words for the same mathematical operation (e.g. add, plus, sum, +, total)?
- Understand numerical relationships (e.g. $3+4=7$ is the same as $7=3+4$ and the same as $4+3=7$ and the same as $7-4=3$, etc.).
- Is a child dyscalculiac if they can carry out the four rules of number but can't do algebra or calculus or geometry or trigonometry?

It might be helpful to consider dyscalculia as it occurs in a syndrome of difficulties. One such syndrome is Gerstmann's syndrome and involves four conditions:

1 an inability to name fingers or to point accurately with eyes closed (finger anomia or finger agnosia);
2 right–left disorientation;
3 poor writing and inability to copy letters (dysgraphia and agraphia);
4 dyscalculia.

It is commonly described in adults who have acquired lesions in the dominant parietal lobe with focal lesions in the angular gyrus (Suresh and Sebastian, 2000). Case studies of developmental Gerstmann's syndrome in children are also occasionally reported (e.g. Garty *et al.*, 1989; Suresh and Sebastian, 2000).

Some researchers view developmental Gerstmann's syndrome as being a specific learning difficulty that is distinct from dyslexia.

Developmental Gerstmann's syndrome	Dyslexia
Tetrad of signs present	Mainly reading and writing difficulties
Not inherited and does not run in families	Could be familial
Poor hand–eye co-ordination	Poor text-scanning skills
Associated constructional apraxia	No apraxia
Severe emotional and behavioural disturbance	Less common/mild hyperkinetic behaviour

In a study of ten children by Suresh and Sebastian (2000), the following descriptions of skills are made:

- Three children were unable to copy any letters (agraphia) and the remaining seven were able to master some writing but had severe spelling mistakes, orthographic errors, substitutional errors, letter omissions and substitutions.
- All had acalculia with difficulty identifying mathematical symbols, simple counting, mental calculations, identifying numbers, simple addition and subtraction and number sequencing.
- All children displayed temper tantrums when any form of writing training was attempted.

Cognitive models for processing numbers

Current models in processing number distinguish between arithmetic facts and calculation procedures (McNeil and Warrington, 1994). One model has been described by McCloskey (1986, 1992), McCloskey *et al.* (1991). An adapted schematic representation is shown below.

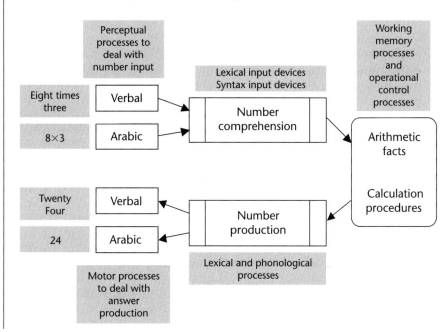

Numerical information enters the model either in written format (Arabic) or in spoken format (Verbal). The numbers are first understood and then converted into some abstract internal representation that can be used in cognitive processes such as calculation. Once an answer is available, the internal representation is converted into numbers that can either be spoken or written down. The semantic processes occurring in the verbal route differ from the Arabic route in that the lexical components are made up of phonological and graphemic components. For the Arabic route, the visual symbolic representation can be converted to meaning by direct access to the lexicon. Syntactical processing involves the processing of the relationship between the elements to understand the number as a whole. For example, the words *six hundred and forty* need to evoke a different meaning to *hundred and forty six*.

Separate processes are included in the model because there are patients who have been selectively impaired in either the verbal or written format. These processes are thought to be double dissociated. There have been reports of patients who could give the correct verbal answer to verbal questions but who could not write it down. Similarly there have been patients who could solve a written problem but not a verbal one.

A 'triple code' model proposed by Dehaene and Cohen (cited in Shalev and Gross-Tsur, 2001) has a neuropsychological and anatomical basis. This proposes three types of representation:

1 verbal
2 visual
3 magnitudinal.

Simple arithmetic operations (including over-learned rote number facts) are processed by the verbal system within the left hemisphere (for most people this is where the language areas are located). More complex operations that require magnitude estimation or visualization are located across both hemispheres. Bardi *et al.* (1998) have shown that in children language disorders such as dysphasia and visual-motor co-ordination disorders such as dyspraxia can affect the development of counting abilities.

Five basic counting principles develop in parallel in children between the ages of 2 and 5:

1 One to One Principle. All objects in a set must be counted once and once only.
2 Stable Order Principle. Numbers used in counting appear in a set order all the time.
3 Cardinal Principle. The last number counted represents the value of the set.
4 Abstraction Principle. Any set made up of distinct elements can be counted.

5 Order Irrelevance Principle. The elements in a set can be counted in any order.

The first principle requires the child to be able to deal with quantity and magnitude. The other principles can be acquired using verbal logic alone.

Ideas for testing and probing

McCloskey's model provides a basis for probing how numerical information is processed.

We can compare inputs with outputs by changing the way a problem is presented to the child and the way that the child is expected to respond:

Problem presentation	Response format required	
Arabic e.g. 4×3=	Spoken verbal	'Twelve'
	Written verbal	Twelve
	Dots	* * * * * * * * * * * *
	Arabic	12
Spoken verbal, e.g. 'Four times three'	Spoken verbal	'Twelve'
	Written verbal	Twelve
	Dots	* * * * * * * * * * * *
	Arabic	12
Written verbal, e.g. Four times three	Spoken verbal	'Twelve'
	Written verbal	Twelve
	Dots	* * * * * * * * * * * *
	Arabic	12
Dots *** *** *** ***	Spoken verbal	'Twelve'
	Written verbal	Twelve
	Dots	* * * * * * * * * * * *
	Arabic	12

This can be followed up with testing of:

- phonological skills;
- working memory skills – this is usually tested using digit span. The results could be confounded by poor number knowledge or difficulty with accessing the number lexicon.

Things to look out for

We can consider the kinds of number processing to look out for in our assessment of children's abilities. The following list is an example (and is not exclusive).

Number knowledge

- rote counting forwards from 1 to 30 (stable order)
- one to one correspondence when counting objects (check on five principles)
- rote counting backwards from 30 to 1
- recognizing digits presented randomly
  - by pointing to digits named
  - by naming digits
- recognizing arithmetic signs
  - pointing to sign named
  - naming signs
- writing digits to dictation
- reading multi-digit numbers
  - getting place names correct (syntax) e.g. thousand, hundred
  - getting value names correct (lexicon)
  - discriminating between symmetrical numbers (e.g. 17 and 71).

Arithmetic facts

- counting forwards in 2s, 5s, 10s
- reversibility in addition (e.g. 3+4 results in the same answer as 4+3)
- multiplication facts – four different rules apply
  - $1\times$ always results in the same number
  - $2\times$ ... $9\times$ rote-learned table
  - $0\times$ always results in zero
  - $10\times$ always results in same number moved up one place
- reversibility in multiplication (4×3 is the same as 3×4).

Procedures

Knows how to complete the different steps to achieve an answer for:
- simple additions (total less than 10)
- additions with totals greater than 10 (carry overs)
- simple subtractions
- subtractions involving 'decomposition' or 'borrow and pay back'
- single line multiplication
- double digit multiplication (e.g. 21×13)
- simple division
- long division
- fractions
- bracketed equations
- simple algebra
- quadratic equations
- etc.

Knows how to apply calculation procedures to different areas of mathematics, e.g. simple geometry to work out the area of a surface:

- deals with regular shapes by dividing into squares and counting each one
- deals with regular shapes by applying multiplication
- has strategies for dealing with irregular shapes
- etc.

The Wave 3 materials developed by the DfES (Gross, 2004) link the key objectives of the National Numeracy Strategy to the types of errors that children make and then make suggestions for remediation and provide the next step in teaching. The key objectives can be used as a skill audit to help identify where a child is in the acquisition of number skills.

Interventions

The following suggestions tackle different aspects of number work in the classroom.

Number and notation

> Naomi is 9 and is still counting on her fingers.

This may not be a problem. It may be that she needs reassurance and favours a tactile approach. There are a number of essential skills that need to be checked:

- Can she count?
- If you start with 21, can she count on to 30?
- Can she count backwards (21, 20, 19)?
- Does she know that 21 is bigger than 19?
- Does she understand that 121 is over 100?

Where pupils have problems with these basic concepts, a range of approaches can be employed to help them develop mathematical skills.

> Sam visualizes numbers and their shape by thinking of a picture, so 'four' is a house with four windows.

Concrete examples are often very helpful if used in conjunction with the written symbols they represent. As with the teaching of literacy, the approach should be multi-sensory: blocks should be examined visually, touched, and moved about in space. For example, if base ten blocks or coins are used, the operations of adding, taking away, etc. can be demonstrated in concrete terms. This is easier for dyscalculiacs than having to deal with two-dimensional symbols on paper.

Pupils need to find what works for them.

> Oliver had difficulty in recognizing the difference between the numbers '24' and '42' and confused similar 'pairs' of numbers. He used a red pen to write the tens and a blue pen for the units and remembered numbers by visualizing the colours rather than their position.

Some pupils cope well with small numbers but once they are over 100 the system falls apart. Learners with dyscalculia often need additional visual or tactile support to embed concepts.

Language and symbols

Once numbers are mastered, we move to symbols and operations. Symbols can be a source of difficulty. Not only are - and ÷ confusingly similar in appearance, but each can be expressed in a variety of ways: 'subtraction' may be expressed as 'less', 'minus' and 'take away'.

'12 take away 7' is the same as 'take 7 from 12', but the pupil may have problems identifying which number is taken from which and how it should be written.

12 divided by 4 may be expressed as:

- 4 divided into 12
- $12 \div 4$
- $\frac{12}{4}$
- 12 shared between 4

All mean the same thing, but learners may not realize this.

The skill of interpreting the special language of mathematics word problems needs to be taught carefully so that pupils can work out exactly what sort of number operation is needed:

'5 girls have 4 toys each. How many toys are there altogether?' (multiplication)

'If Nadim runs for 15 minutes and William runs for 5 minutes less, how long has William been running?' (subtraction)

Children must be able to recognize *when* to multiply two numbers in a problem and *which* two numbers should be multiplied; that only comes with an increased understanding of mathematics and what you are trying to do. The Numeracy Strategy suggests that learners be allowed to make up their own word problems from number statements. Doing this can help the dyscalculiac understand the language of mathematics and how it is translated into formulae.

Quite a lot of teachers make a symbol sheet or, even better, get the

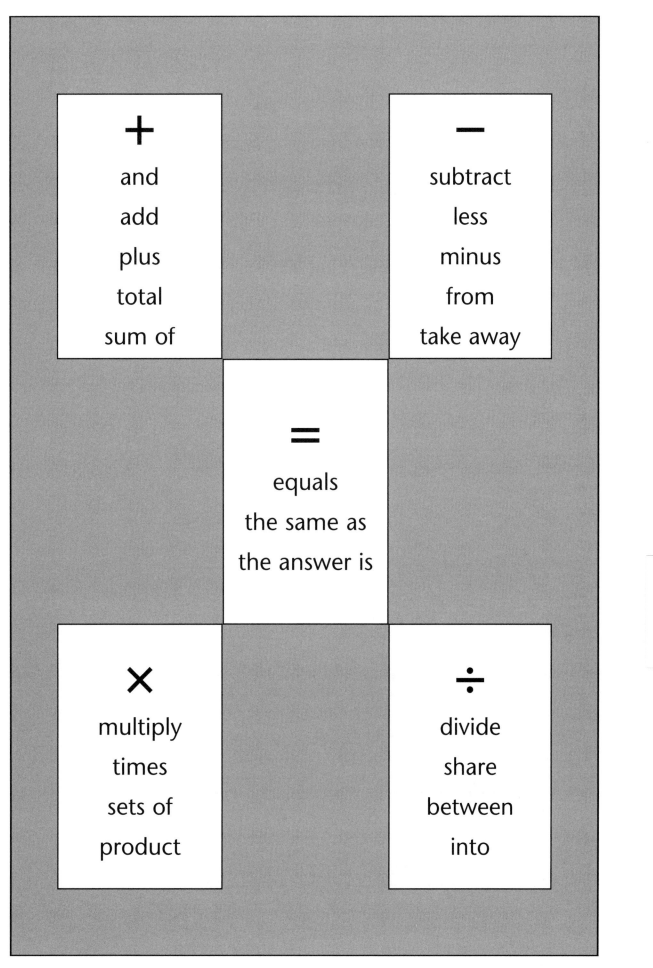

pupils to make their own as they go along so that each symbol is associated with particular vocabulary. It gives the learner a chance to practise the symbols and to have a prompt that they can refer to. The symbol sheet that Michael built up over a period of time, as he came across particular phrases, is shown on page 117.

Number bonds and learning tables

Again, look for visual and tactile approaches. Use puzzles, games, construction equipment, calculators and software to help with number bonds and tables.

The BDA has a really helpful information sheet, which can be downloaded from http://www.bda-dyslexia.org.uk/d09maths/index. htm

It shows tips and hints for the 9 and 11 times tables, and how to draw a table square that is a ready reckoner for tables. By giving pupils a quick and easy guide to tables on paper you are supporting those who learn visually – learning by rote is an auditory method.

Calculators

Ofsted produced a report in 2002 based on inspectors' observations of mathematics lessons and discussions with pupils in 68 schools. They expressed concern at the limited use of calculators:

> *Despite its value the calculator is not a regular feature in the teaching of the daily mathematics lesson at Key Stage two (pupils aged seven–11). A significant number of teachers refer to its use but do not give it enough emphasis. When it is used, teachers give too little attention to encouraging a range of options, such as using mental methods ... alongside the calculator.*
> (Ofsted, 2002)

Of course, a calculator is no substitute for good teaching, but some learners find that a calculator has proved a useful aid, not just to getting an individual answer right but, through repeated use, to learning particular products or number bonds.

> Sofia can't tell the difference between '4005' and '405'. She writes '405' as '400' then adds on the '5' (4005).

Sofia's teacher needs to check if she knows the difference between hundreds and thousands and whether the problem is with the concept or just the notation (how it should be written). Sometimes a talking calculator can provide a breakthrough. Sofia would type in '4005' and it says 'four thousand and five'. This lets her know at once that she has got it wrong. The alternative is that she hands in her work to the teacher, waits for it to be marked and then gets it back a few days later, when she has forgotten what she was doing. The calculator is a tool in helping her take responsibility for her own learning.

Patterns

Sometimes learners work so slowly that they never discover patterns or make sense of what they are doing. They don't always realize that a particular exercise contains increasingly complex examples of the same type of activity. Using a calculator to practise number bonds or place value can be helpful. Many teachers and parents think that using a calculator is cheating, but it can help pupils speed up and recognize patterns.

Gareth and Robert were using a calculator to learn about multiplying and dividing by 10. During the lesson they operated on more than 20 decimal numbers. They made tables in their books showing the starting numbers and the answers.

.315	3.15	31.5
5.6	56	560
11.27	112.7	1,127
0.05	0.005	0.0005

When they had discovered the rules, they predicted the answers for a few more numbers and used the calculator as a check. Then they added extra columns to their table and kept trying different sums, exploring multiplication and division by 100, 1,000 and other powers of 10.

Without the calculator, Robert and Gareth would probably have spent the entire lesson doing six calculations and getting two of them wrong! There is no possibility that they would have discovered any pattern.

Estimation

Reasoning is the basis of estimation and a problem-solving approach. These are skills that are just as important as basic knowledge. In fact, they may be even more crucial for those with specific learning difficulties since they may help them to overcome problems with memory, transferring skills and assimilating information.

Estimating and checking are vital skills for everyone, but they are especially significant for this group of learners who are often accustomed to being wrong and can easily become discouraged. Motivation can be a real problem with a learner who is intelligent enough to realize that they are underachieving and yet cannot find a way to improve their skills. By estimating answers they can begin to take some measure of responsibility for their own work.

These skills need to be developed in various ways: some pupils need a carefully structured programme of moving from the simple to the complex. For others a breakthrough seems to occur when real-life parallels are used.

> Adrian is trying to work out 98 miles at 34.2p per mile. He uses a calculator and comes up with 3351.6. He writes down £3351.6 but then realizes that no one would claim that much money for a car journey. This helped him to see the point of estimating. 'Nearly 100 miles; 100 pennies in a pound so it's nearly £34.'

Ways of working

It is often thought that dyscalculiac learners are not 'poor learners' but 'quick forgetters'. The National Numeracy Strategy may be helpful to them in a number of ways:

> *The structure of the NNS provides frequent returns to topics allowing pupils to review and reinforce previous learning. Dyslexic pupils will greatly benefit from opportunities to overlearn. However, asking them to produce answers quickly, either mentally or written, will disadvantage most dyslexic learners.*
> (BDA, 2001)

The whole emphasis for pupils with dyscalculia needs to shift from writing to doing, from memorizing to understanding, from looking to touching and moving:

- Let them learn by doing and then learn how to write it down.
- Make use of pictorial representation, number lines, table squares for number concepts and counting.
- Don't impose solutions; discuss what works for them and find ways of building on it.
- With older learners, make sure that the materials are appropriate to their age and interests.
- Link skills to real-life situations, simulations based on shopping, catering or travel, for example.

> Gary had problems remembering different topics if he had not worked on them for a few weeks. Revision was a nightmare because he seemed to be approaching topics for the first time, often with limited success. He found that a small notebook with a worked example for each topic, which he could refer to every week, helped to keep the subject in his head.

It is essential to minimize verbal explanations. If the learner is given a sequence of spoken instructions before carrying out a task, he can be doubly handicapped. First, short-term memory may be at fault so one instruction may be omitted and secondly, since sequencing is a problem, he may get the order wrong.

Possible solutions:

- Let the pupil write down each step as he finishes it.
- Provide a scribe to write down what a pupil is doing, for future reference.
- Provide a written set of notes prepared by the teacher.
- Encourage the child to practise each step until it is embedded in his memory.

Siobhan is quite competent at mathematics now but was always in the remedial group at school. She realizes that the main problem was the way new topics were introduced.

'The teacher would explain it and give us an example on the board. If I didn't understand, he would come and explain it again. I could always follow the first bit but got lost somewhere in the middle. He would explain it three or four times and each time he'd phrase it a bit differently. In the end there was a great fog of words in my head and I still didn't know what I was supposed to do. He'd say, "Do you understand it now?" and I'd say, "Yes, thank you." I was too embarrassed and too confused to go through it again.'

What about a computer program?

Generally, the computer can help in the following ways:

- It is associated with enjoyment.
- It provides a welcome change in presentation.
- It does not criticize, nor condemn.
- It has endless patience.
- It can provide extensive practice in numeracy skills.
- It can do many basic calculations, especially using spreadsheet, graph and statistics programs.
- It can improve presentation.

Programs need to be selected with care, taking into account the pupil's age, the presentation of the program and the level(s) and topics of work available.

Software may help both in the classroom and at home, but beware of using software just 'because it is fun'. Similarly, tedious drill and practice is still tedious if it is on-screen.

Some programs such as *Intellimathics* are good tools for developing investigations about numbers. It has sorting activities and counting boxes with base ten blocks. Pupils move and manipulate objects, so it is a bridge between handling counters and coins on a table and the more abstract skill of writing down numbers on a piece of paper. Pupils move the mouse around the screen and, in some cases, this helps them to concentrate. Many programs work on a 'what if ...' basis. 'What if I double the number?' 'What happens when I change the figures in this spreadsheet?'

It is not possible to suggest software for each topic and stage here, so use these guidelines to make an informed choice.

Choosing software

- Does it teach or provide practice and over-learning?
- Do the tasks test understanding rather than just memory?
- Does it have rewards or penalties, and if so are these a useful feature or a distraction?
- Are there visual cues on the screen to help learners work out answers?
- Are the screens clear and uncluttered?
- Is it clear what the learner has to do?
- Is there audio support?
- Does it need high-level literacy skills?
- Does it provide a chance to explore and experiment? Does it encourage a 'what if ...' approach?
- With older learners, make sure that the materials are appropriate to their age and interests. Using software with pictures of toys just adds insult to injury!

Summary
- Mathematics is a symbolic language.
- Pupils may have problems with digit and symbol recognition.
- Not all dyslexic learners find mathematics difficult; some excel in this area.
- It can be useful to minimize verbal explanations.
- Try a range of approaches. Let the pupil move and manipulate objects, use colour, learn by doing and then learn how to write it down.
- Get pupils to make their own symbol sheets.
- Use a calculator to speed up work and to reinforce patterns.
- Remember that estimating and checking are vital skills.
- Beware of using software just 'because it is fun'; make sure it teaches skills instead of merely providing tests.

7 | Emotional Support

The emotional needs of a child with dyslexia are just as important as, if not more important than, academic development. Some parents worry that the frustrations of not being able to deal with print or to record ideas will lead to depression and to an increased risk of:

- being bullied
- strong feelings of inadequacy
- feelings of failure
- feelings of shame and embarrassment
- suicide.

Charlton (1992) suggests that the emotional response of the child will become more significant with age. The experience of failing to read leads to demotivation or emotional blocking. This in turn leads to the child avoiding reading and reduces the expenditure of effort and persistence in trying to read. This then leads to a reduction in reading experience and less success compared to peers. The child sees the gap between themselves and their peers appear to get wider, and this increases their emotional response further eroding self-esteem.

The cycle continues, leading to what Stanovich (1986) calls the Matthew effect: good readers get comparatively better while poor readers get comparatively worse. Poor progress for SpLD (specific learning difficulties e.g. dyslexia) pupils in secondary schools in reading development has been attributed to poor self-esteem, low self-confidence and experience of failure with literacy in primary schools (Ofsted, 1999). This means that the emotional impact of dyslexia cannot be ignored. In some studies, working on self-esteem through counselling has been shown to be more effective in improving reading skills than spending the same time on remedial teaching (Lawrence, 1985).

A number of emotionally supportive strategies are discussed throughout this book. In this section, we will consider understanding emotional responses and particular techniques to support specific emotional responses.

Emotional responses

Our emotional responses in any situation depend upon how we interpret what is happening around us. This in turn depends upon our previous experiences. If dyslexic children have a history of struggling with reading then it is not surprising to find that they often react quite strongly when presented with a reading task. The way in which they interpret the presenting task will affect the type and strength of emotion that they experience. This in turn will help to determine how they behave.

Experience
(Stimulus)

Cognitive appraisal based on bodily reaction, facial expressive responses, evaluative feelings, action tendencies

Emotional
affect

Behaviour
(Response)

The appraisal of the situation happens very quickly and we are often not aware of the contributing thoughts. Such thoughts are referred to as automatic thoughts and lead to the activation of a whole range of responses (see the figure above).

Jane is asked to read out in class. An automatic thought flashes through her head so quickly that she is unaware of it, 'I'm useless at reading'. Her physiological system becomes activated with an increase in heart rate and release of adrenalin – the fight or flight hormone. Cognitively she thinks, 'I'll probably make mistakes and the other kids will laugh'. She becomes motivated to avoid the situation, 'If I get sent out I won't have to do this'. Emotional responses might include feeling ashamed or even angry that the teacher is putting her through this ordeal. She may even think that the teacher hates her – why else would she make her feel like this? Further evaluations of the situation might lead her to notice David smiling. Another automatic thought enters play, 'He's laughing at me'. This leads to the behaviour – verbal or physical abuse of the child who smiled. This is the behaviour the teacher sees and Jane is sent out of the room.

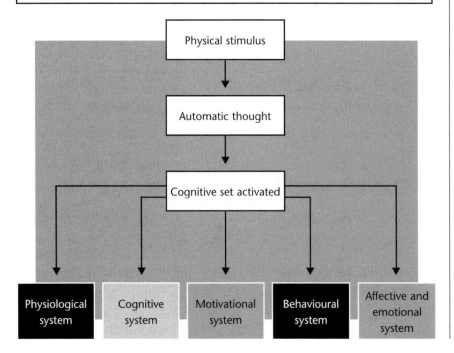

Cognitive set activation (Squires, 2001b, 2002)

Supporting Children

The child can be supported by helping them become aware of automatic thoughts. The relevance of the automatic thought to the current situation can then be checked out and alternatives offered. *What else could David have been smiling at? Perhaps he was laughing at you, perhaps he was pleased to see you were chosen. Maybe, he was smiling at the girl behind you. Perhaps he was pleased because the teacher had just said how pleased she was with his reading.* The child is taught to ask a series of questions to check out their response:

- How do we know which possibility is true?
- How can you find out? What evidence can you get?
- How would you feel in each case?
- How strongly?
- What would you do in each case?

Emotional blocking

Emotional blocking occurs when a task is presented that is well within the child's ability but the child considers it to be too difficult and reacts against that possibility by withdrawing from the situation. These strategies will help pupils to deal with the emotional blocking that leads to their reluctance to work through a problem or answer a question:

- Encourage risk-taking with prompts to the child, e.g. 'have a go', 'what's your best guess?'
- Encourage risk-taking in the classroom ethos, e.g. modelling that it is OK to make mistakes.
- Ask pupils to rate their confidence in knowing the answer. Then ask them for their answer and then for their rating again. If their answer is correct, use feedback to challenge the pupil's low self-evaluation. For example, 'You gave yourself 2/10 for being sure that was the right answer – and your guess was right!'
- Use bridging techniques. For example, ask the pupils to think of other examples where they have known the answer – 'This is a bit like the problem with the sinking and floating ... what happened when I put the wood in water? How might that help us here?'
- Spend some time on class exploration of problems that have no 'right' answer to show that there are several possibilities rather than simply right or wrong.

Encouraging pupils in the search for solutions

Strong emotional responses such as anger and frustration are expressed by some pupils when things seem to be out of their control. Other pupils respond by withdrawing or apparently giving up. Engaging pupils in the search for solutions to perceived difficulties is helpful because it starts to bring the situation more into their control.

Open-ended questions

An open-ended starting point can be found by asking pupils how things might be different. Some children find this type of phrasing difficult and might find other open-ended questions easier, such as:

A genie appears and grants you three wishes. What would you ask for?

Once the pupil has started to express what he would like to be different, the task then becomes one of trying to create the steps to get there. How many solutions can you generate?

Paul: *I wish that I could read.*
Teacher: *You wish you could read better?* [Reframe and reflect.]
Paul: *Yes.*
Teacher: *If it happened tonight, what would you read tomorrow?* [Make the discussion specific.]
Paul: The Lord of the Rings
Teacher: *Wow! That's a big book – lots of people like that. Who might help you?*

This discussion might then lead into a number of possible solutions:

- paired reading with a more able peer;
- an apprenticeship approach with a parent;
- whole-class reading of the text;
- work on particular parts of the text with a teaching assistant;
- looking at an illustrated version; or
- making a personal version using a computer to write key phrases and adding drawings to make it into a book.

Rating scales

A simple scale of 1 to 10 (or 1 to 100) can be used to ask a pupil to identify the degree of a problem in different situations or over time. For example, Steven has problems with his work; he often does not complete the task set. He is asked to rate each subject:

Teacher: *On a scale of 1 to 10, 10 being really good and 1 being terrible, tell me how much work you are able to do in each subject.*
Steven: *English 5; maths 4; PE 10; science 5; history 8; geography 1 ...*

Once this task is completed there can be a focus on the subjects that have low scores:

Teacher: *What makes geography so difficult that it only scores a 1?*
Steven: *There's too much writing. I get lost when I am copying.*

The search for solutions then continues by looking at those subjects that score higher.

Teacher: *What happens when you are copying in science?*

Steven: *The teacher gives us a worksheet and I can put my ruler under the words that I have to write – I don't get quite so muddled and don't have to keep checking where I am up to.*

Teacher: *And in history – you gave that a high score – what helps there?*

Steven: *Well, the teacher tells us to do the work, then she comes round to make sure we're all doing it. Sometimes, when we copy off the board, she writes each line in a different colour. Often we have a sheet to stick in our books and we just fill in the gaps or write the answers to the questions.*

A number of solutions start to become apparent:

- having the target text near to where Steven is copying allows him to use his ruler as a tracking aid;
- different coloured writing on the board helps with tracking;
- sticking worksheets into his book helps him keep up;
- being checked on helps him to start the work and not waste time at the beginning of the task.

With the last point, Steven could be empowered to help him engage with self-checking. He could be encouraged to see how well he can start his work in each lesson. A simple self-rating scale could be used for him to write on to photocopies of his weekly timetable:

1 – took ages to start; 5 – so-so; 10 – started straight away

Transitions

Transitions are simply changes from one class to another, from one school to another, or from one Key Stage to another. Transitions and change always provoke anxiety. This is natural; we all feel like this to some extent as we move from the safety of what we know and are comfortable with towards the unknown and unpredictable. Parents and children have many worries about what might happen or might not happen. The key transition that all pupils make is from primary school to high school and this often causes the most worry for parents.

Some secondary schools have started to run summer schools for pupils who are transferring and who might have a weakness in literacy or numeracy. The intention is to provide additional teaching so that pupils are better able to cope with the secondary school curriculum and organization.

Preparing for change

Preparation for moving to secondary school should start early on in Year 6. The primary school and secondary school are likely to have

Callum is due to transfer to the High School in September. His mother is quite concerned that this placement will not succeed. She is worried that:

- *he won't be able to read the text;*
- *the pace of work will be much faster;*
- *the level of work will be much harder;*
- *it is a big school and teachers will not know him as well as they do in his small primary school;*
- *he will not be able to find his way around;*
- *he will forget what to take with him each day;*
- *there will be a lot of writing to do;*
- *he won't be able to cope with tests and examinations;*
- *homework will be difficult.*

established procedures that will make the transfer of information efficient. The main problem will be that parents may not have decided on their choice of secondary school at this stage. The first task for parents is to visit possible secondary schools in order to make that decision during the autumn term.

As part of the initial visits, parents should seek out key people who will be able to support their child:

- SENCo
- head of Year
- Form tutor (if known at this stage, though this is not normally decided until the summer term).

During the spring and summer terms further visits can be made to the school. Try to visit the secondary school when the school is working so that you and your child can:

- experience what lessons look like;
- see the range of work done (practical as well as writing);
- experience the vastness of the secondary school building;
- experience the crush in the corridors at breaktime;
- look to see where things are (e.g. toilets, break facilities, clubs, canteen);
- meet key people again so that the child will have a friendly face they can turn to.

All this is important in reassuring the child that his basic needs will be met and enabling him to look forward to starting at the new school.

During the summer term, link teachers from each school meet and share important information about special needs and strategies used to support the pupil. Many schools operate a system of visits for the pupils transferring so that they can spend some time with their new teachers and become familiar with the school layout. In some schools incoming pupils are paired with pupils already in Year 7 and a pen-pal relationship is nurtured. This can be especially valuable if two dyslexic pupils can get together to share concerns and insights.

Some secondary schools have screening procedures for pupils entering the school. These may include reading tests, spelling tests and verbal and non-verbal reasoning tests to help identify children with special educational needs (including high ability), and provide a useful baseline against which to measure progress. Pupils with dyslexia may need to be reassured about these tests if they are not to constitute a bad start to secondary education.

Bullying

Some children are worried about bullying, and there may be many myths about what will happen to the new Year 7 pupils in September. It is a reality that bullying occurs in all schools (and in many workplaces). All schools are required to have established policies for dealing with bullying. Some schools have other strategies to help and these include:

- Buddy systems – where older pupils befriend new pupils, usually in a structured way at first. In some schools, pupils are identified as 'buddies' on a rotational basis and will be available to pupils at breaktimes or lunchtimes.
- Peer mentoring systems and peer counselling systems – which operate in some schools where older pupils have received training from organizations such as Relate.

When parents are worried about potential bullying they should:

- Work on past experience – if their child was not bullied at primary school then there is no reason to suppose that they will necessarily be bullied at secondary school. If they were bullied at primary school then how was the problem resolved? How will that help to resolve issues which might arise in the future (if they arise in the future)?
- Talk to teachers at the secondary school to see how they might be able to help. They may have more specific resources to help, e.g. some schools now have trained counsellors.

Summer schools

Summer schools are run by some secondary schools and aim to improve basic literacy and numeracy. They provide a number of other opportunities:

- A chance to get to know some of the school staff before the pressure of term starts. Most primary school teachers are female and the move to a secondary school will provide some pupils with their first encounter of male teachers. This can have a positive effect by providing a male role model in a school setting.
- A chance to start to develop advanced study skills such as:
  - mind-mapping
  - note-taking
  - working with ideas when writing, planning, reviewing and editing.
- Time for school familiarization, which is made easier when the school is almost empty, 'orienteering' games and map-making activities, which are useful preparation for the start of term.
- Time for games to encourage:
  - team building

- thinking skills
- problem-solving skills
- improving co-ordination (brain gym).
- Teaching children strategies for everyday organization, and encouraging good habits, e.g. spot prizes for having a pencil, ruler and eraser.

Summary

Emotional difficulties arise from a variety of sources and can lead to demotivation, emotional blocking or even more extreme reactions when a child is faced with print.

- Understanding how these emotional responses arise can help parents and teachers work with the child to overcome them (or even prevent them in the first place).
- Pupils can be encouraged to search for solutions as equal partners, using open-ended questions and rating scales.

Transitions are a particularly difficult time for parents and children alike. They can be made easier through:

- adequate preparation for change
- good links between key staff
- summer schools.

---

8 | The Parents' Role

For many parents it comes as a great shock when their child fails to make satisfactory progress in reading at school. Often the child has been good with language in the home and has learnt to speak early. Many dyslexic children have been very articulate and have picked up and used words and phrases that are way beyond their years. They have enjoyed being read to and have a good memory for the fine details of stories.

Harry was a bright child who learned to speak early. He was articulate and funny and picked up and used words and phrases that were way beyond his years. He enjoyed being read to and had a good memory for the fine details of stories. He loved Dear Zoo and Mrs Plug the Plumber and would join in, shouting: 'Send for Mrs Plug! … When Mrs Plug was sent for, Mrs Plug came.' He loved songs and rhymes and often recalled catchphrases from television programmes or the refrains of songs he had not heard for some months.

Harry had no problems with memory, no learning disabilities and had a love of the intricacies of language. His mother noticed that he did not recognize written words as quickly as his older sister, but reassured herself that every child is different and Harry would soon catch up when he got to school.

Like many children, Harry looked forward to going to school and his parents had no particular anxieties. He was bright and sociable and had enjoyed playgroup and nursery. When parents see their child's friends coming out of school with higher-level reading books, however, a certain unease or competitiveness creeps in. Why are they forging ahead? They think: 'Perhaps if my child spent more time reading and less time watching TV, he would be as good.' So before long there is the nightly battle over reading. The child begins to sense he is not quite up to the mark and wants to avoid the issue; the parents are determined to help the child to catch up. Progress is minimal or even non-existent and everyone in the house is sick of reading the same text night after night. Sometimes the child knows the book off by heart but cannot recognize the individual words out of context. He has an excellent memory but, whatever is happening, it's not reading. A deficit model sets in. Instead of the child being known as the one who is funny, or good at football or who has a great singing voice, he begins to be known as the child who cannot read, who is a problem and a worry to his parents. It doesn't have to be like this. On page 133 we will start to look at what parents can do. Before that, let us take a moment to look at other aspects of the same problem.

The disaffected child

As the child gets older he realizes that he is in a special group, often with children who are not good at learning in general. What they come to realize, however, is that they can have a good time together and, the more outrageous they are, the more they make other children laugh. Here is something they are good at.

Girls are just as likely to have dyslexia as boys, but boys are far more likely to be identified for special help in schools. It is unclear why this is the case, but one factor may be the perception of reading and writing as a 'girly thing' and the ensuing lack of interest by boys. If girls take more of an interest in books and stories, playing at post offices and writing in their Barbie diaries, the foundations of literacy skills are already being built. In most cases they will have strong role models of mums and grans reading to them, writing shopping lists and sending notes to the teacher. This gender stereotyping is reinforced in primary schools where most of the staff are women. Reading can become a female occupation in the eyes of some boys. Their teachers and their mother seem to have an obsession with reading and writing and doing well at school. Girls take trouble with their work and produce nice neat projects, go to the library and find information, but boys play football, or hang out with their mates and try to get by. As time goes on, it seems more of an uphill struggle; they will never get there so why bother?

Boys lag behind in early literacy skills and later on in English. The gap is apparent as pupils enter school for the first time and remains sizeable throughout pupils' primary schooling and into the secondary stages. Recent Research on Gender and Educational Performance, *1998, The Stationery Office.*

Sometimes children hang on to this mind-set and, before long, they are getting into trouble at school and on the streets, and in adolescence end up with a criminal record. Young offenders' centres and prisons have a disproportionately high number of dyslexic inmates. Sometimes the child follows a different route and becomes very dependent and clingy, constantly seeking reassurance and telling everyone he meets that he is dyslexic.

Young offenders' centres and prisons have a disproportionately high number of dyslexic inmates. Dyslexia affects between 4–10% of the population. 52% of the randomly selected offenders showed strong indications of dyslexia. The London Offender Study, *1998, www.literacytrust.org*

Sometimes, in an attempt to protect and support their children, parents unintentionally exacerbate the problem. One young man told me that his parents arranged after-school sessions with a private tutor and Saturday morning specialist classes. His diet was carefully regulated as they had heard about the effect of E-numbers on concentration. No squash, no crisps, no sweets, no birthday cake or treats that other children enjoyed. He saw his lack of reading skills as his parents' problem. He functioned perfectly well without being able to spell; he disliked reading and saw it as a waste of time when he could be out on his bike or going fishing.

What can you do?

First of all, try to stay calm and avoid making it an issue. Think to yourself, 'Is this a real problem or might my child catch up?' Talk to teachers at the school. Sometimes parents have unrealistic expectations and compare their own child unfavourably with the most talented readers and not with the average child, so they overreact. Of course we all want our children to excel but not every child is a bookworm – some will have talents in languages or mathematics, sport or art. Many children develop skills relatively late, so if a child is not a fluent reader at the age of 6 it is not necessarily time to worry. Be guided by your child's teacher who will alert you to any concerns she may have about lack of progress. Schools usually begin to plan support strategies for a child when, after several terms in school, he demonstrates any or all of the following difficulties. He:

- cannot recognize and remember early 'key words';
- has difficulty in writing his own name correctly from memory;
- does not identify the 'initial sounds' of words; for example, he cannot say that 'baby' begins with a 'b', or cannot play 'I-spy';
- cannot pick out an 'a' or 's' from a selection of plastic letters;
- finds it hard to re-form simple words made of plastic letters, when the letters are jumbled up (e.g. 'sit', 'mat', 'pig').

As children get older, many schools use reading ages (RAs) as a measure of progress. As a rule of thumb they take an RA of two years less than chronological age (CA) as an indication of significant difficulty. (If a child is 9 years old and has an RA of 7, he would usually be identified for extra support.) The tests used to establish an RA can give differing scores, however, and it is often better to trust an experienced teacher's assessment – especially with young children. (See the table on page 30.)

At the end of Key Stages, reading and writing will be assessed by SATs (Standard Assessment Tasks) in a way that compares each child with his peers and against the 'norm'.

Reading

Read together. This might sound obvious, but many parents spend time hearing their child read their reading book night after night but do no other reading together. Get the schoolbook out of the way in ten minutes. It needs short, regular practice but it is not the most motivating reading activity. Choose books from the library together. Don't worry if the book your child chooses looks babyish – it is his choice. Similarly, if the book is too hard for him to read, you can read it together. Try a bit of paired reading each day. Either you read a sentence and then your child reads the next one, or you read out loud together so that he can hear the words as he looks at them (see the guide on page 135).

Paired reading can be a delicate process with older readers. They will benefit from the practice but care should be taken not to make them feel 'babyish'. They may prefer to use non-fiction books – perhaps tied in with a homework task or lesson content. Poetry can be a good choice, especially when humorous, and has the advantage of being in short, manageable 'chunks'.

Talk about the story. So often, reading can become just a 'decoding' exercise where you work out each word but don't get the whole picture. Talk about what you have read during the day so that reading is seen as a normal activity and not a big hurdle which your child cannot overcome. As your child gets older and begins to read silently, try to read the same book as them from time to time. It takes only a short amount of time to read a slim children's paperback and will give you an opportunity to discuss the story with your child, what you (and he) liked and disliked about it, etc. This is an excellent motivator for developing readers – if an adult takes the time and trouble to read a book then it must be worth reading. Having one-to-one time together is also a reward in itself – especially if the discussion is kept light-hearted and fun.

Keep reading to your child. If he enjoys 'classics' such as *Treasure Island*, or is hooked on *Harry Potter*, these books are not easy reads. Reading to him will help him to finish the story in a reasonable time and keep up his interest. Many children enjoy being read to long after their transition to secondary school. Buy, or borrow from the library, story tapes (talking books) and encourage your child to play them on his personal stereo while waiting at the bus stop or travelling in the car.

Paired reading

- Start with the book closed. Make sure your child holds the book, or place it on the table in front of him, rather than you 'having ownership'.

- If this is a new book, ask your child what they think the story is about. Look at the title and the author. If it is a picture book, you may look at some of the pictures before starting to read – this will create a context for the story and 'cue-in' the reader.

- If you are continuing to read a book, ask your child: 'What happened last time?'

- You may need to gently remind him of the storyline. Use this time to set up some expectations – 'What do you think will happen?'

- Specific questions can be used to link previous reading with the new reading and pull the story together.

- Now open the book and read quietly together.

- Sometimes, you will take the lead. Sometimes, your child will lead.

- If your child struggles with a word, do not worry. Simply count to five in your head then tell him the word. The pause should give him a chance to work it out, but not be so long that it disrupts the flow of the story, or makes him feel embarrassed.

- Make a mental note of words that were difficult and use these (another time) for word-building practice or precision teaching.

- At the end of the reading, close the book and ask the child a few questions to see how much he has understood and remembered.

- Ask him what he thinks might happen next, what he would do if he was the main character, etc.

- It can be valuable to give the child an opportunity to re-read a passage from time to time. Having practised the text and worked out any difficult words, the re-reading gives him a chance to practise fluency and expression – and to enjoy it! This works especially well with dialogue, where the reader can concentrate on the 'voices' and have some fun.

Writing

If you have a computer, get your child to use it. Make posters, put on borders and experiment with fonts. Make it fun.

See if your computer will talk. If you have a sound card and can hear the sound effects on CD-ROMs, your computer has the capability to support synthetic speech. The easiest way to do this is to buy *textHELP: Read and Write 2000*, which sits on top of *Microsoft Word* and can be set up to read out loud as you type, or to read the whole document. It also provides full-screen reading of text, menus and icons. Be prepared for your child to type in lots of rude words to start with as the computer will read anything! However, the novelty wears off quite quickly. Children can also copy entries from CD-ROMs or web pages and get them read aloud so they improve their listening skills and auditory memory, learning to get information from the spoken word.

Quick writing projects

1. You are going to make the most disgusting pizza in the world. Write your shopping list.
2. Tales from Viking Days – choose a colour and font to make an attractive title.
3. Make a football poster.
4. Write a Valentine's Day card.
5. Produce a menu for your favourite meal.
6. Write a list of ten things you could not live without.
7. RED: make a list of all the things this colour suggests to you – sunsets, postboxes. Find the font colour tool. Write them all in red and choose a different font for each.
8. Camping in Wales, clubbing in Tenerife or safari trekking? Make a poster for your ideal holiday.
9. Devise a board game and write up the rules.
10. What wild animal would you choose to adopt? Use the web to find facts and pictures and write an appeal to be published in a magazine.

Spelling

Start with games:

- *Syllable spotting.* Many children have little idea of syllables. Explain that a syllable is a name for a beat. How many beats are there in these words: 'him', 'music', 'Superman'? Tell them each beat has at least one vowel ('a', 'e', 'i', 'o', 'u'). Sometimes, 'y' acts as a vowel (in words such as 'my' and 'shy').

textHELP!® Systems Ltd
Enkalon Business Centre
25 Randalstown Road
Antrim
Co. Antrim
BT41 4LJ
N. Ireland
Tel: 02894 428 105
Fax: 02894 428 574
http://www.texthelp.com
Also available from Semerc (www.semerc.com) and Inclusive Technology (www.inclusive.co.uk).

- *Word building.* Help them build phonic words (words that are spelled as they sound).
- *Use your word processor.* Make 'wordworms' like this one –

ItwasadarkandstormynightwhentheshipsetsailfromDover.

Get your child to use the space bar to put in the spaces. This helps with word recognition and reading.
- *Make 'word hunts'.* This is particularly useful when your child has lots of new vocabulary and spellings to learn. This is some of the vocabulary needed for history: burghers, gentry, nobles, serfs, peace, war, victory, defeat, treason, traitors, rebellion, riot, prisoners, punishments, branding, pillory, stocks, beheaded.

History 'word hunt' made with the SPA program

Use squared paper or, on the computer, make a grid in Word using *Tables*. Put in the words and then add extra letters around them, leaving some blanks if you need to simplify the task. Alternatively, you can buy a program called Word Square Maker from SPA that will do all the hard work for you and will create several different versions so the same words can be practised again and again.

SPA Ltd
PO Box 59
Tewkesbury
Gloucestershire
GL20 6AB
Tel: 01684 833 700

Wordsearches can be fun, but some youngsters will find them laborious, so be guided by your child. Using lower-case letters makes the words easier to recognize than using capitals.

Learning spellings for homework can be stressful for all concerned. Parents are anxious to 'do their best' for their child; the child is under pressure to perform and not let his parents down. The task itself can be boring and very difficult for a dyslexic child. All this and, at the same time, parents may have two or three other children to attend to, a meal to prepare and ironing to finish. The pointers on page 138 may be helpful.

If you find that learning spellings is taking a disproportionate amount of time and/or causing your child a lot of distress, it is worth speaking to his teacher or the school's SENCo about the problem. In some cases, a decrease in the number of words to be learned will solve the problem. There is no reason why every child in class has to learn the same spelling list every week.

If you are working on spellings:

- Keep it short – 10 minutes each night or in the morning four or five times a week is much more effective than 40 minutes one night and half an hour at the weekend.

- Start a session with one or two spellings from the previous night/week or words that you know the child will get right. This builds confidence.

- If there is a long list of words, split them up into one or two at a time: move on at the child's pace.

- Use a multi-sensory approach. Look at the word, say the word, break it up into syllables, single sounds or letter names – whatever works best for your child. Write the word – in the air, on each others' backs, with your eyes closed and in joined-up writing if possible as this creates a tactile 'pattern'.

- Now ask your child to have a go at writing the word by himself, without a model.

- Is it correct?

- If it is – great celebrations! Pile on the praise. Come back to the word in 10 minutes, then half an hour, then an hour – to practise and reinforce the spelling. This can be done in the commercial breaks, while washing-up, in the bath, etc. Be light-hearted about it.

- If your child is still having difficulty, ask him to spell as much of the word as he can and leave out the tricky bit. It can help to provide your child with the right number of letter spaces.
  For example, if the word is 'going', jot down the letter spaces _ _ _ _ _ then ask him to have a go: 'g o _ _ g'. 'Well done, you're nearly there. Let's look at the tricky bit.' In this case, you can say, 'The missing letters spell a tiny word on their own, look, "in". Let's practise them on their own. Now, put them into the bigger word.'
  With more difficult words, a mnemonic might help (see page 144).

Secondary pupils

What about older children?

Some parents worry that their child will not cope at secondary school where they have new subjects, including modern foreign languages. They have to move from room to room, may have no class base, have to remember which books to take on which day, and deal with a variety of teachers.

Some parents transmit their anxiety to their children, so that far from the transition to big school being a time of excitement, it becomes an ordeal. In fact, many boys do better at secondary school. It seems as if they mature as more is demanded of them. Perhaps having male teachers makes a difference to their perception of school. Also, some of the secondary school curriculum has more 'boy appeal'. Many boys avoid drama and English but enjoy more practical subjects such as business studies, design and technology, ICT and sports. In 2002, 80,000 boys opted for GCSEs in PE, compared to only 37,000 girls. It may be that new subjects do not carry the taint of failure.

You can still work on spellings together. Many parents buy books of spellings but this is not necessarily helpful as they are likely to contain words the child will never use. You need to focus on words your child is already using. Look for the language they need for different subjects. Look in their exercise books to see which words are causing problems.

If subject-specific vocabulary is becoming a problem, you could ask the subject teacher for a list of words needed for a particular topic or term's work. Being able to prioritize these *in advance* of needing them will be a great benefit. Sometimes the teacher will be happy to provide a copy of the textbook for this purpose, though these may be in short supply in some schools. Alternatively, go through the SENCo who will be able to approach the subject teacher on your behalf – or even do a 'trawl' of several subject departments. Be patient! These are busy people, but they should recognize the benefits that will come from taking the time to provide you with this information.

Jenny has a daughter, Carla, in Year 8.

'She was getting more and more depressed about her spellings and her work always seemed to be covered in red ink. She used to write out the words over and over again using Look-Cover-Write-Check, but it didn't stick. If she didn't use the words for a few weeks, they would go again.

One night I went through her work and picked out about 50 spellings. Most of them were quite common words. Some of them had similar patterns so I put them together. We did five to ten minutes each night after tea. I would write the word out correctly and we would talk about what she was getting wrong and how she could learn it. Sometimes we found a little word in a big word. She used to write "tradgedy" but then we found "rage" in the middle so she remembered that.

They were doing business letters at school. She used to put "buisness" but when we talked about it and she saw it was from the word "busy" – "busi" + "ness" – it made more sense. She couldn't write "sincerely" but when we split it into "since" + "rely" and talked about how you rely on a sincere person, she got it. I realized that a lot of the time she made haphazard guesses about words. Once she could link a spelling to other words she knew she got on much better.

These little "tricks" worked for Carla but probably wouldn't work for another child. You have to know the child really well to find the things that work. That's where it helps if you are family because you have so many shared experiences you can tap into.'

Summary
- Get out more! Try to develop a range of interests that you and your child can enjoy together which do not focus on reading and writing.
- Make sure your child has opportunities for physical activity. Some parents report that sport – especially swimming or dancing – seems to improve reading skills.
- Consider diet, but don't be over-cautious. Provide a good balanced diet with plenty of fresh foods, but also the range of chocolate, crisps, etc. that other children are allowed.
- Read to your child and try paired reading instead of insisting on your child reading to you. Take turns or read together so the child hears and sees the words.
- Make writing fun. Use the design features on a word processor. Make the computer talk. Let your child see you writing – and having to look up spellings from time to time.
- Don't lose sleep over spellings! Play Scrabble and other games. Make jokes about awkward words. Help your child to come to terms with his difficulty, while working on ways for him to improve.
- Take your time. Little and often is the best recipe. Stop if tempers get frayed. Try for ten minutes, five times a week, as this shows the best results.
- Encourage independence. Help your child to do things for themselves and then stand back and let them try it out. Every time they organize themselves, they become more confident. If they fail, you should not take over but discuss how they can do better next time.
- Stay positive! Easier said than done, but do try. Do not hover anxiously, make negative comments or show that you think your child will fail.
- Find something to praise your child for – every morning and every evening.

9 | Dyslexia and Me

When you were told you were dyslexic, how did you feel? Were you worried that you'd never be any good at reading and writing? Were you relieved because it explained why you had problems? Were you delighted because it meant you were gifted? Not many people see it as a gift at first. They have been told for so long that they are bad at things and can't keep up with the class – but this doesn't have to be you!

Look at this list of famous and talented people. They built on their strengths and took the world by storm. Obviously having problems with the written word didn't hold them back.

Entertainers Cher Whoopi Goldberg Eddie Izzard	**Poets** W.B. Yeats Benjamin Zephaniah	**Actors** Tom Cruise Dustin Hoffman Steve McQueen Jack Nicholson Anthony Hopkins
Writers Hans Christian Andersen Agatha Christie	**Musicians** John Lennon Beethoven Mozart	**Film directors** Quentin Tarantino Walt Disney Steven Spielberg
Inventors Albert Einstein Henry Ford Thomas Edison Alexander Graham Bell Leonardo da Vinci	**Politicians** Winston Churchill Benjamin Franklin John F. Kennedy	**Sportsmen** Carl Lewis Duncan Goodhew Jackie Stewart Magic Johnson

These people found what worked for them. They had imagination and an ability to think and do things in a different way. That's what made them stand out from the crowd.

Recognizing your difficulties

Is this you?

- Some days, language is no problem, but on other days you can't put your ideas into words.
- You probably talk better than you write.
- Sometimes you read but don't get any meaning from it.
- You 'drift off' while reading.
- You may have lots of different spellings for one word.
- You're not good at proof-reading because you don't spot that what you've written is not what was in your head.
- When you listen you don't get a sense of what is said; and you have problems coping with more than a couple of instructions at a time.
- You can get words in the wrong order when speaking.
- You have problems organizing yourself and your time.
- You often turn up with the wrong equipment for lessons.

What can you do about ...?

Organizing yourself

- *Imagine yourself doing things.* If you have swimming tomorrow, imagine getting your swimming gear out of a drawer or the airing cupboard, wrapping it in a towel, finding a comb and shampoo and putting the whole lot in a bag. The more detailed the picture, the more likely you are to do it.
- *Have a large plastic box with a lid* to keep vital documents in. This becomes more important as you get older and have to keep track of chequebooks, letters, university applications, forms and your driving licence.
- *Make lists.* You don't have to write in words, you could use pictures or symbols. It saves you cluttering your mind with trivia.
- *Repeat things.* When someone gives you a list of instructions, say them out loud and in your head. Sometimes hearing your own voice can help to fix them in your mind.
- *Use 'Post-it notes'* to jot down things you think of on the spur of the moment. Stick them to the wall or door if you cannot deal with them at once. If you are at school stick them to the inside of a folder or exercise book.
- *Buy some brightly coloured folders* in which you put handouts, etc. Try to pick colours that are linked to the subject in your head, e.g. green for geography because it's about the earth.
- *Pack your schoolbag the night before.* You forget less if you are NOT doing it at the last minute.

Left and right

- Hold up both hands as in the picture below. Look at the shape made by your thumbs and first fingers. The one that makes the shape of an 'L' is your Left hand. If this doesn't work for you, try wearing a Ring on your Right hand.

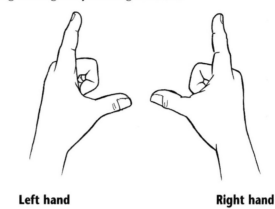

Left hand   **Right hand**

Reading

- *Read something every day* – even if it is the back of a cereal packet or an email. The more you read, the easier it will be for your eyes to cope with print.
- *Try out filters.* Ask your school if they have any. Try out different colours to see if they make reading more comfortable.
- *Ask your teachers to photocopy handouts on to different coloured paper* if this helps you.
- *Get a talking word processor* on your computer at home, if you have one. You can copy stuff off the Internet and CD-ROM entries into *Word* and it will read it out to you.
- *Get the video or audiotape* for books you are studying in English literature. Watch or listen to the whole thing before you start reading. That way you will know the gist of the story and be able to take in more detail as you read.

Writing

- *Think about using mind-maps for planning.* You can sketch them on a piece of paper or use a program such as *Kidspiration* to create them. Look at these two pieces of writing about elephants. Which is easier for you?

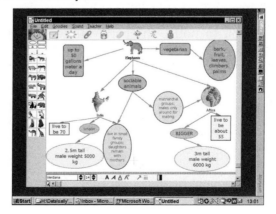

- *Try to plan, then create, then correct.* If you worry too much about spellings in the early stages, you'll never write anything.
- *Record your ideas on tape,* if this helps.
- *Look at the design* of various pages; does the font used make a difference to you? Make your own set of samples by choosing different fonts – style, size, colour – on different coloured backgrounds. You can change the colour of the paper and the text very easily. Go to the *Format* menu on the Tool bar and click on *Background*. Choose the colour. Try these options:

- blue text on a yellow background,
- black text on a blue background, or
- red text on a blue background.

Spellings

- *Decide which words you want to learn to spell.* If you need them, and use them a lot, you are more likely to learn them.
- *Try to write the words.* Get a friend/parent/teacher to write the correct spelling at the side of your page. Pick out the part that you get wrong and write it in capital letters or in a bright colour. For example:

'yesterday'   'yesterday'   'yes**TER**day'

This helps you to notice the part you get wrong. Your eye is drawn to the correction and you are using your visual skills to remember it.

- *Develop mnemonics.* This is probably one of the hardest words to spell! It is pronounced 'nem-on-icks' and means 'an aid to memory'. For example, you can make up a sentence that spells a difficult word:

A right **i**diot **t**hought **h**e **m**ight **e**at **t**offee **i**n **c**hurch = arithmetic
Big **e**lephants **c**an't **a**lways **u**se **s**mall **e**xits = because

144

- *Find little words in big words, e.g.*

  'listen' = 'lis' + 'ten'
  'intermittent' = 'in' + 'term' + 'it' + 'tent'

- *Learn rules*, e.g. 'after "suc", "ex" and "pro", double E must go'. This means that 'succeed', 'exceed', 'proceed' and 'precede' are all correct.
- *Use a cassette recorder.* Say the word, spell it, then leave a pause. Listen to the tape as often as possible and repeat the spelling during the gap on the tape. After a while, the spelling will be second nature – as you think of the word, you will start reciting it.
- *Use a spell checker on your computer.* Look at the words it suggests. Keep a list.
- *Use a handheld spell checker* such as a *Franklin SpellMaster*. Type in your version of the word and see what it suggests.

Find out what you are good at

It is all too easy to get fed up and think that you will never overcome your difficulties. You might feel that your parents and teachers are only interested in your reading and spelling and are not interested in you as a person.

You can make some changes. Try to identify the things you are good at. No one can be good at everything. Tick the boxes on page 146 to show the things you are good at. Spaces have been left empty for you to write in your own ideas. You could ask people who know you to say what they think you are good at.

Summary
- Many famous people are dyslexic and gifted.
- Make sure you know and celebrate your strengths.
- Read something every day, even if it is just a cereal packet.
- Get organized. Use files and folders for school work and a large box for important documents.
- When you have a lot to remember, sit and think about what you need to do. Imagine you are doing it.
- Be colourful! Use coloured folders for different subjects. Try coloured overlays for reading. Use different background and text colours on the computer.
- Be active about spellings. What words do you need to know? How will you learn them? You can use look-cover-write-check; you can split the word into syllables and exaggerate the sounds, you can look for little words in big words or you can develop your own silly sentences to help you remember.
- Be noisy! Say spellings out loud. Talk through what you are going to do and how you will do it. Use tape recorders to make voice notes or to practise composing. Use a computer with a talking word processor.

What am I good at?

Art and drawing	
Acting and drama	
Remembering information	
Discussing ideas	
Science and investigations	
Making friends	
Helping people	
Sport	
Speaking languages	
Singing	
Cooking and making up recipes	
Finding my way around	
Number work and mathematics	
Music	
Telling jokes	
Telling stories	
Playing computer games	
Looking after animals	
Spotting bargains in the shops	

Think about what you do well. How did you learn it? Can you apply this method of learning to other areas at school or at home? How do you want people to remember you? You need to show people what you are good at – if you don't tell them they won't know. Above all, celebrate all your successes, you've earned them!

References

Audit Commission (2002) *Policy Focus. Statutory Assessment and Statements of SEN: In Need of Review?* Wetherby: Audit Commission Publications.

Bardi, A., Laquière, C., Fayol, M. and Lacert, P. (1998) Pathologie du dénombrement: approche d'une dyscalculie développementale. *Annales de Réadaptation et de Médecine Physique* **41**, 499–502.

BDA (2001) *M01: Dyslexia, Dyscalculia and Mathematics.* British Dyslexia Association, September.

Braundet, M., Molko, N., Cohen, L. and Dehaene, S. (2004) A cognitive characterization of dyscalculia in Turner Syndrome. *Neuropsychologia* **42**, 288–98.

British Psychological Society (1999) *Dyslexia, Literacy and Psychological Assessment: Report of the Working Party.* Leicester: BPS – Division of Educational and Child Psychology.

Brooks. G. (2002) *What Works for Children with Literacy Difficulties? The Effectiveness of Intervention Schemes.* RR380. London: DfES.

BSA (2000) *Literacy and Numeracy: What Adults Can and Can't Do.* London: Basic Skills Agency.

Bulstrode, C. and Hunt, V. (2000) What is mentoring? *The Lancet* **356**, 1788.

Charlton, T. (1992) Giving access to the National Curriculum by working on the self. In Jones, K. and Charlton, T. (1992) *Learning Difficulties in Primary Classrooms: Delivering the Whole Curriculum.* London: Routledge.

Cooper, P. and McIntyre, D. (1993) Commonality in teachers' and pupils' perceptions of effective classroom learning. *British Journal of Educational Psychology* **63**, 381–99.

DfEE (undated) *How can I Tell if a Child may be Dyslexic? Handy Hints for Primary School Teachers.* London: DfEE.

DfES (2001) *Special Educational Needs Code of Practice.* London: DfES.

DfES (2002) *What Works for Children with Literacy Difficulties? The Effectiveness of Intervention Schemes.* London: DfES.

DfES (2005) *Every Child Matters: Green Paper.* London: DfES. See also www.everychildmatters.co.uk

Garty, B., Waisman, Y. and Weitz, R. (1989) Gertsman Tetrad in Leopard Syndrome. *Pediatric Neurology* **5**, 391–2.

Gross, J. (2004) Tracking children's learning charts. The materials discussed here have now been developed into a package of materials for schools called *Supporting children with gaps in their mathematical ability* (DfES ref 1168-2005 G) and can be downloaded from www.standards.dfes.gov.uk/primary/publications/inclusion/wave3pack/

[The] *Guardian* (1998) Living by the word – even when you can't always read about it. 5 November.

Heaton, P and Winterson, P. (1996) *Dealing with Dyslexia*. London: Whurr.

Henderson, A. and Chinn, S. (2004) Dyslexic pupils and the key objectives of the National Numeracy Strategy. In Reid, G. and Fawcett, A. (eds) *Dyslexia in Context: Research, Policy and Practice*. London: Whurr.

Jordan, I. (2000) *Visual Dyslexia: Signs, Symptoms and Assessment*. Desktop Publishing: http://www.visualdyslexia.com

Kullman, J. (1998) Mentoring and the development of reflective practice: concepts and context. *System* **26**, 471–84.

Landerl, K., Bevan, A. and Butterworth, B. (2004) Developmental dyscalculia and basic numerical capacities: a study of 8–9-year-old students. *Cognition* **93**, 99–125.

Lawrence, D. (1985) Improving self-esteem and reading. *Educational Research* **27** (3) 194–9.

Lovegrove, W.J. (1994) Visual deficits in dyslexia: evidence and implications. In Fawcett, A. and Nicholson, R. (eds) *Dyslexia in Children: Multidisciplinary Perspectives*. New York: Harvester Wheatsheaf.

Lovegrove, W.J. and Williams, M.C. (1993) Visual temporal processing deficits in specific reading disability. In Willows, D., Kruk, R. and Corcos, R., (eds) *Visual Processes in Reading and Reading Disabilities*. Mahwah, NJ: Lawrence Erlbaum Associates.

McCloskey, M. (1986) cited in Grafman and Boller (1989).

McCloskey, M. (1992) Cognitive mechanisms in numerical processing: evidence from acquired dyscalculia. *Cognition* **44**, 107–57.

McCloskey, M., Harley, W. and Sokol, S.M. (1991) Models of arithmetic fact retrieval: an evaluation in light of findings from normal and brain-damaged subjects. *Journal of Experimental Psychology: Memory and Cognition* **17**, 377–97.

McCrone, J. (2002) Dyscalculia. *The Lancet Neurology* **1**, 266.

McNeil, J.E. and Warrington, K. (1994) A dissociation between addition and subtraction with written calculation. *Neuropsychologia* **32**, 717–28.

National Numeracy Strategy (2001) DfES document 0286-2004.

Neale, M.D. (1997) *Neale Analysis of Reading Ability – Revised: Manual for Psychological Services.* Windsor: NFER.

Nicholson, R.I., Fawcett, A.J. and Dean, P. (1995) Time-estimation deficits in developmental dyslexia: evidence of cerebellar involvement. *Proceedings of the Royal Society of London. Series B-Biological Sciences* **259**, 43–7.

Nicholson, R.I., Fawcett, A.J., Berry, E.L., Jenkins, L.H., Dean, P. and Brooks, D.J. (1999) Association of abnormal cerebellar activation with motor learning difficulties in dyslexic adults. *The Lancet* **353**, 1662–7.

O'Hare, A.E., Brown, J.K. and Aitken, K. (1991) Dyscalculia. *Developmental Medical Child Neurology* **33**, 356–61.

Ofsted (1999) *Pupils with Specific Learning Difficulties in Mainstream Schools: A Survey of the Provision in Mainstream Primary and Secondary Schools for Pupils with Statements of Special Educational Needs relating to Specific Learning Difficulties.* London: Ofsted Publications Centre.

Ofsted (2002) *Teaching of Calculation in Primary Schools: A Report by HMI*, HMI 461. London: Ofsted Publications Centre.

Ofsted (2003) *The National Literacy and Numeracy Strategies and the Primary Curriculum.* London: Ofsted Publications Centre.

Questions Publishing (2004) *SEN: A Classroom Guide.* A series of information sheets published with *Special Children.* Birmingham: Questions Publishing.

Rack, J. (1994) Dyselxia: the phonological deficit hypothesis. In Fawcett, A.J. and Nicholson, R.I. (eds) *Dyslexia in Children: Multi-disciplinary Perspectives.* Hemel Hempstead: Harvester Wheatsheaf.

Rennie, A.G. (1996) Assessments of deficits in visual functioning. In Harding, L. and Beech, J.R. (eds) *Assessments in Neuropsychology.* London: Routledge.

Schlaug, G., Jancke, L., Huang, Y. and Steinmetz, H. (1995) *In vivo* evidence of structured brain asymmetry in musicians. *Science,* **267** (5198), 699–701.

Selfridge, O.G. (1959) Pandemonium: a paradigm for learning. *Mechanization of Thought Processes.* London: HMSO.

Shalev, R.S. and Gross-Tsur, V. (2001) Developmental dyscalculia. *Pediatric Neurology* **24**, 337–42.

Shiel, G. (2002) Literacy standards and factors affecting literacy: what national and international assessments tell us. In Reid, G. and Wearmouth, J. (eds) *Dyslexia and Literacy: Theory and Practice.* Chichester: John Wiley.

Squires, G. (2001a) An evaluation of a booklet of ideas to support teachers in reflecting on the strategies used when teaching dyslexic children. Unpublished research project submitted in part fulfilment of the requirements of the doctorate in educational psychology. University of Manchester.

Squires, G. (2001b) Thoughts, feelings, behaviour: helping children understand themselves and take more control of their behaviour. *Special Children* **134**, January.

Squires, G. (2001c) Dyslexia friendly. *Special Children* **142**, November/December.

Squires, G. (2002) *The Theory and Practice of Cognitive Interventions.* Ainsdale: Positive Behaviour Management.

Squires, G. (2003) Cognitive preferences and spelling. Unpublished research project submitted in part fulfilment of the requirements of the doctorate in educational psychology. University of Manchester.

Squires, G. (2004) Supporting children with ... *Special Children* **158**, 21–9.

Stanovich, K., (1986) Matthew effects in reading: some consequences of individual differences in the acquisition of literacy. *Reading Research Quarterly* **21**, 360–406.

Stanulis, R.N. and Russell, D. (2000) 'Jumping in': trust and communication in mentoring student teachers. *Teaching and Teacher Education* **16**, 65–80.

Stein, J.F. (1994) A visual defect in dyslexics? In Fawcett, A. and Nicholson, R. (eds) *Dyslexia in Children: Multidisciplinary Perspectives.* New York: Harvester Wheatsheaf.

Stein, J.F. (1996) Visual systems and reading. In Chase, C.H., Rosen, G.D. and Sherman, G.F. (eds) *Developmental Dyslexia: Neural, Cognitive and Genetic Mechanisms.* Maryland: York Press.

Stein, J.F. and Talcott, J.B. (1999) Impaired neuronal timing in developmental dyslexia: the magnocellular hypothesis. *Dyslexia* **5**, 59–77.

Stein, J.F., Richardson, A.J. and Fowler, M.S. (2000) Monocular occlusion can improve binocular control and reading in dyslexics. *Brain* **123**, 164–70.

Suresh, P.A. and Sebastian, S. (2000) Developmental Gerstmann's Syndrome: a distinct clinical entity of learning disabilities. *Pediatric Neurology* **22**, 267–78.

Ta'ir, J., Brezner, A. and Ariel, R. (1997) Profound developmental dyscalculia: evidence for a cardinal/ordinal skills acquisition device. *Brain and Cognition* **35**, 184–206.

Treiman, R. (1997) Spellings in normal children and dyslexics. In Blachman, B.A. (ed.) *Foundations of Reading Acquisition and Dyslexia: Implications for Early Intervention*. Mahwah, NJ: Lawrence Erlbaum Associates.

Turner, M. (1997) *Psychological Assessment of Dyslexia*. London: Whurr.

Waldie, K.E. and Mosley, J.L. (2000) Hemispheric specialisation for reading. *Brain and Language* **75**, 108–22.

Wechsler Objective Reading Dimension (WORD) (1993) London: The Psychological Corporation.

Williams, M.C. (1999) Faculty webpage, University of Louisiana. Retrieved on 1 March from http://www.neuroscience.lsumc.edu/faculty/williams.html

Useful Contacts

Barnaby Blackburn's personal site – www.iamdyslexic.com

Becta – www.becta.org.uk

The Bristol Dyslexia Centre – www.dyslexiacentre.co.uk

British Dyslexia Association – Tel: 0118 966 2677; www.bda-dyslexia.org.uk

British Dyslexics – www.dyslexia.uk.com

Department for Education and Skills – www.dfes.gov.uk

Dyslexia in Scotland – www.dyslexia-in-scotland.org

dyslexia-information.com – www.dyslexia-information.com

The Dyslexia Institute – Tel: 01784 463 851; www.dyslexia-inst.org. uk

Dyslexia parents resource – www.dyslexia-parent.com

Dyslexia Research Institute – www.dyslexia-add.org

Dyslexia Research Trust – www.dyslexic.org.uk

Dyslexia teacher – www.dyslexia-teacher.com

The International Dyslexia Association – www.interdys.org

NASEN – Tel: 01827 311 500; www.nasen.org.uk

The National Grid for Learning – www.ngfl.gov.uk

Supporting Children Series

These books are ideal for both teachers and learning assistants in specialist and non-specialist settings. Each book provides theory about a specific need, plus practical advice, support and activities to facilitate children's learning.

Orders

All these titles are available from your local bookshop, but in the event of any difficulty please order directly from us.

Orca Book Services
Stanley House
3 Fleets Lane
Poole, Dorset
BH15 3AJ, UK

Tel: +44 (0) 1202 665 432
Fax: +44 (0) 1202 666 219
E-mail: orders@orcabookservices.co.uk

For ordering information inside North America, please call 1-800-561-7704.

(PHOTOCOPY AND USE)

SUPPORTING CHILDREN WITH ADHD

2nd Edition

Kate E. Spohrer

A collection of practical suggestions and materials to use with pupils who have ADHD or demonstrate ADHD-type behaviour. This new edition is enhanced by two new chapters: one on the theory, medication and alternative therapies for ADHD, and one covering what the teacher can do, including case studies, an Individual Education Plan (IEP) writing guide and reflective questions for the teacher about the child and teaching strategies.

May 2006 * 112pp * Paperback * A4
0 8264 8077 2 * **£17.50**

(PHOTOCOPY AND USE)

SUPPORTING CHILDREN WITH DYSLEXIA

2nd Edition

Garry Squires and Sally McKeown

Supporting Children with Dyslexia focuses on the practical difficulties facing dyslexic pupils every day in the classroom.

This second edition now offers even more information, particularly on the definitions of dyslexia, perceptual issues, spelling patterns, remedial programmes, useful techniques, and dyscalculia.

May 2006 * 160pp * Paperback * A4
0 8264 8078 0 * **£17.50**

(PHOTOCOPY AND USE)

SUPPORTING CHILDREN WITH SPEECH AND LANGUAGE IMPAIRMENT AND ASSOCIATED DIFFICULTIES

2nd Edition

Jill McMinn

This book describes how these difficulties can adversely affect children's learning in both specialist and mainstream settings and suggests how the curriculum can be made more accessible to facilitate learning.

This new edition has been fully updated and now includes a photocopiable, task-based assessment chapter, and a suggested structure for Individual Education Plans (IEP) together with a template and bank of possible targets.

May 2006 * 192pp * Paperback * A4
0 8264 9103 0 * **£20.00**

continuum

Continuum International Publishing Group Ltd • London and New York • www.continuumbooks.com